THE MOWER BOY

AN AUTOBIOGRAPHY OF
ROGER F. GREIN

AS TOLD TO: CLAIRE ANN PATTERSON

WESTBOW
PRESS®
A DIVISION OF THOMAS NELSON
& ZONDERVAN

WestBow Press books may be ordered through booksellers or by contacting:

WestBow Press
A Division of Thomas Nelson & Zondervan
1663 Liberty Drive
Bloomington, IN 47403
www.westbowpress.com
844-714-3454

ISBN: 979-8-3850-3216-7 (sc)
ISBN: 979-8-3850-3218-1 (hc)
ISBN: 979-8-3850-3217-4 (e)

Library of Congress Control Number: 2024917778

Print information available on the last page.

WestBow Press rev. date: 09/12/2024

The Mower Boy

An Autobiography of Roger F. Grein

Founder and President of Magnified Giving,
Philanthropist, Entrepreneur, Speaker, Coach,
Man of Faith, Mentor, Leader and Friend to all he meets.

I dedicate this book to my loving parents, Frank and Thelma Grein.

photo of Frank and Thelma Grein

I also dedicate this book to the four people who first
suggested that I write a book about my life:

Sister Anne Brennan, CSJ
Sister Janice Brewi, CSJ
Father John Ferone, SJ
Sister Therese Martin Hessler, SFP

CONTENTS

CONTENTS

ACKNOWLEDGEMENTS

I would like to thank the following people who have contributed to this book:

Claire Patterson, my friend and co-author

Kathy Thamann, Mary Ann Gronotte and Susie Curtis for editing assistance

Patricia Bethell for interior art

Michael Brocker for technical assistance

James W. Jackson, Julie Ciocci and Mark Soeder for testimonials

Kelly Collison and Jeanne Hunt for advice and encouragement

FOREWORD

I first met Roger in 1993 while serving as the Director of Development for Xavier University in Cincinnati, Ohio. In my field, one has the opportunity to meet many people who make a difference in the world. All these caring people have inspired me and have provided me with stellar examples of generosity and character. But there is one man who has gone far beyond these qualities, and has etched an indelible mark on my mind, heart, and soul.

Roger is a modest man with a long history of generous giving. No one realized or knew of his true generosity to numerous causes. His humility lent comfort to being in the background.

As we became close personal friends, I realized that so much of who Roger is has evolved through his life experiences. Roger grew up with the physical challenges of cerebral palsy. Although he could never competitively play sports, Roger served as an assistant manager for every team his high school fielded. He took challenges head on and learned the value of perseverance, dedication, and genuine care for others.

He graduated from the University of Cincinnati in only three years with a Finance Degree, and earned his MBA in night school. Roger had two degrees, but could not find a job because of his poor handwriting; the result of cerebral palsy. After returning to his steadfast lawn cutting customers from his youth, and turning mowing clients into tax clients, he was doing 345 tax returns and became the tax commissioner for three local municipalities. In 1970 he opened his own tax and accounting company with, eventually, eight employees.

While I was serving at Xavier University, Roger developed a unique program of student service-learning. He visited many colleges and introduced students to the concept of philanthropy. His vision was to teach youth how to research, invest and support community non-profits. With the help of the Ohio Campus Compact, Roger transferred administration of Ohio's 34 college programs in 2006 and it evolved into the "Pay It Forward" program on 1,100 campuses.

In 2008 Roger's investments (90% in bank stocks) plummeted. His portfolio shrank dramatically from $7 million to $65 thousand. He was obliged to inform the non-profits he cherished that his ability to give had greatly diminished. When he lost his money, Roger was devastated; not for himself but for all the organizations to which he had promised money.

He shared this great sadness with me, but true to Roger and his ever-positive attitude, faith, and desire to change lives, he was ready to take a new path. He came up with a vision and dream to establish a non-profit that would inspire, engage, and educate high school students and magnify the impact of their philanthropy to help the community.

His non-profit, *Magnified Giving*, was launched in that same year of 2008. Roger introduced his concept to eight pilot schools at the secondary level. It was here Roger's life experiences, connections, and desire to do good, flourished. Herein lies the brilliance of Roger's extraordinary innovation: a new concept to support non-profit organizations that provides six times the impact of a benefactor's investment. Here is how it works:

1. Benefactors invest money into Magnified Giving.
2. Magnified Giving awards qualifying schools the opportunity for their students to become involved in experiential learning.
3. Qualified teachers are selected and trained to become coaches.
4. Students are provided the opportunity to serve as philanthropists, researching non-profits and acting as investment managers of this money.
5. Students select award-winning non-profits to receive the grant money, which will serve to support the non-profit's mission.

6. The deserving recipients of the non-profits then distribute the finances to help support their mission of helping others in their program.

Magnified Giving at its finest! This is an amazing program that impacts today, yet carries on into the future to assure philanthropy's future. This is a perfect match of mission, vision, and a way to educate our next generation to lead meaningful lives of responsibility and giving.

To date, Roger, through Magnified Giving, has educated over 45,000 students to prepare them to become non-profit board members, donors, volunteers and change makers in the community. During the 2023-2024 school year, 136 programs impacted 5,737 youth and funded 152 grants, totaling $202,223. BUT, historically, it is impressive and relevant that Roger's nonprofit has empowered over 45,000 youth and they have awarded $1,780,416 in grant dollars to 640 non-profits since 2008.

From my own personal perspective, Roger has had a profound impact on my life. Over the years, Roger has transformed from an acquaintance, to benefactor, to friend, to mentor and to saint. I have heard the saying, "A friend is someone who reaches for your hand, but touches your heart." I can attest to this reality in my life through this outstanding man.

Roger displays unconditional love, eyes that see, and a heart that gives. He has a "can do" demeanor with a passion to do God's work as he is called to do. Roger is unique, original and one of a kind.

Everyone knows and loves Roger, from the city mayor to the young waiter seating him at the restaurant. Goodness comes to Roger, and he returns this goodness back to the world *magnified*. He is the spark in everyone's heart that invites and ignites their purpose and optimism for a better world, providing them strength and encouragement through his daily living example.

Sincerely,

James W. Jackson

INTRODUCTION

In 1999, I attended three religious retreats. During those retreats I shared some of the struggles I had encountered in my life and how I managed to maintain a thankful attitude. Four of those retreat leaders (Father John Ferone SJ, Sister Therese Martin Hessler, SFP, Sister Anne Brennan, CSJ and Sister Janice Brewi, CSJ) all suggested to me that I write an autobiography. They believed that others could learn from my trials and triumphs.

I had never considered such an endeavor. I am not a writer; nor am I a reader. To be honest, I haven't read a book since college. I enjoy the sports pages in the newspaper - that's the extent of my reading for pleasure. I am a guy who likes numbers. So, I was taken aback and daunted by their suggestions to write a book about my life experiences.

After mulling over their recommendations, I began to think that perhaps these four inspirational leaders often make that sort of remark to others. I sought out each one individually, and asked, "With how many people have you made the same suggestion?" They each told me, "I've never said that to anyone but you, Roger."

I took it to prayer. "God, if you really want me to write a book, you are going to need to send me some help!"

Shortly thereafter, a Sister of Notre Dame de Namur recommended a writer to me. When I called the man she referenced, we talked about the project at length. He agreed to come to my house once a week for two years. He patiently listened to me talk, and put it down on paper. He was a gift from God; he was an answer to my prayer.

It was like taking the road to Emmaus. God took care of me; He was walking beside me. Very few people have the opportunity to write the story of their lives, and without God's help, it would never have happened.

By 2001 we had written three complete drafts for the book; all of varying lengths.

We began looking for an agent that could take one of these drafts to a publisher. We were almost ready to sign a contract with an agent in 2008, when the financial tsunami of Wall Street hit me hard. All of the money I needed to complete the process was gone.

In the end, I had nothing left to show for our efforts but a file cabinet full of manuscripts. So many intangibles - so much work – evaporated! You can't put a price on that! I had to say good-bye to the writer and shut down the process of getting the book published.

Sixteen years later I heard from an old acquaintance.

Claire Patterson and I had known one another from St. James' Church. We met in 2006 when we both attended daily Mass and prayed our rosary before services. I told her my story over a couple of breakfasts, and she suggested I write my autobiography. Claire said she was in the process of writing a book, and would be happy to work with me on my book at the same time. I told her that I had already hired a writer to help, but thanked her for her offer. Then, I gave her the audio recordings of two of my radio interviews. One CD was labeled, "The Mower Boy" which, I told her, was intended to be the title for my autobiography. We lost touch a few years later.

In January 2024, Claire, probably prompted by the Holy Spirit, decided to listen to "The Mower Boy" CD again. After the recording ended, she wondered what had ever happened to my book, so she began looking for it online, hoping to buy a copy. When she couldn't find it for sale on the Internet, she began searching for me by name. She found the website, "Magnified Giving," which provided a way for her to send a message to me. She wrote that she would like to buy my book. I called her back and told her I had never published the book. She offered her help completing my autobiography and we agreed to meet at our Magnified Giving office.

Our first meeting was fun. Claire called it a "treasure hunt." We searched through a cabinet, stored inside a closet in one of our meeting rooms. We found several pieces of the original chapters, and a few complete manuscripts. We both realized that since the last pages had been written in 2001, twenty-three years earlier, there was much more story to be told. She took a manuscript home, and began working through it.

We had several meetings after that day, and you are holding the result of the work by Claire, several volunteers and myself.

Aware that everyone is confronted by obstacles in life, the goal of this book is to encourage each reader to overcome them, as I have done, and continue to do.

I hope you enjoy the story of my life, and pass this book on to others. May God bless you and guide you through any difficulties and set-backs you encounter. Don't let unexpected hardships stop your initiatives. Ask God for His help!

I pray that you count each challenge as an opportunity to love God and those people close to you in your life. Never give up. Never lose your hope and never lose your faith in God.

Blessings, Roger

CHAPTER 1

REVELATION PART I

I was forty-eight years old when I first heard my original name.

I was driving my father back from a chemotherapy treatment. He sat in the back of my car, and my mother was in the front on the passenger side. We came to a stop light, when my mother, looking absent-mindedly out her window said, "That was your name."

I looked over at a sign. It said, "Wang."

"That was your name," she said again. "Joseph Michael Wang." Then she added wistfully, "Maybe you have money."

That was the end of the conversation. She didn't turn her head or say anything more; the light turned green and I pulled away.

That five-second comment was the first time either of my parents had, in over forty years, mentioned to me anything about my previous identity. It was also the last time. My father died the following year, and my mother developed Alzheimer's a few years after that.

"Joseph Michael Wang," she had said. It would be another eight years before I learned anything more about my family history.

∼

There is a Cathedral in Cincinnati, Ohio that sits next to the City Hall building. Both edifices have spires visible from all over downtown and from Interstate 75, as it leads north to Detroit and south to the Ohio River and Kentucky.

1

Most of the time the Cathedral sits in a kind of splendor; gleaming, quiet, high on a rampart of concrete steps, its front doors closed to the noise of downtown.

In an older ten-story office building, shoehorned between the towers of the Cathedral and City Hall, is a building referred to only as "100 East Eighth."

On the eighth anniversary of my father's death, in 1999, I had an early morning appointment in this building. I was now fifty-seven years old and about to embark on a journey I had never taken.

That morning, I had attended 7:00 a.m. Mass and then picked up Joyce, my office manager, and Dianne, a good friend. I had asked them to join me on this adventure of discovery, because I needed trusted companions with whom to share this momentous event. And besides, I had a hacking cough and no voice left. I required someone to speak for me and take good notes.

I thought about Mom and Dad and how they would feel about this investigation into my past. Would they have been hurt? Would they have thought that all they had given me had not been enough?

In my pocket I had a receipt in the amount of $3.75 from the Hamilton County Probate Court for an adoption fee. I also had my birth registration and a letter dated April 13, 1943 from Catholic Charities. It testified that, as babies go, I was in perfect condition. Boy, did they miss the mark with that report! I patted my pocket to make sure these three documents were still safely tucked away. They were the only paper trail I had.

The path to this moment was intentional, but not planned. I had not set out deliberately upon this journey of investigation, but had instead made a few casual inquiries regarding my past. I was an accountant, business owner and softball coach with an often-relentless schedule. I didn't have the time, or even the desire, to throw myself into finding my biological family, or the identity that might have been mine. During the past September, completely by accident, one such casual inquiry had pierced the proverbial bull's eye. I had noticed an article about a woman who found the son she had long ago given up for adoption. There was mention of a lady who had helped her find the lost son. Fortunately, this helpful lady's email address was included in the article.

I had never visited the World Wide Web and had, of course, no email address at that time. Such stuff was as alien to me as calculators and microwaves were to the generation before me. I tore the article from the paper and handed it to a friend. He got in touch with the woman in the article, who in turn called me. She asked a few questions and then directed me to the Catholic Social Services of the Archdiocese of Cincinnati. I learned from this source that anyone born before 1964 could access records about their birth. A few calls later, and I was on my way.

I had actually contacted Catholic Social Services twenty years earlier; even before the death of my father. It was a spur-of-the-moment visit. I was getting older and probably just realizing some new aches here and there. I wanted to know if there was any pertinent medical history, within my biological family, I should know about. While I was there, I also asked if I could leave a note for my birth mother, in case she should ever want to reach me. I wanted to tell her how grateful I was for the life she had given me. With a stone face, the social worker disappeared for a few moments, then returned, only to say there were no medical records available. That was all the information she shared with me. She then dismissed me, and proceeded to speak to the next person in line.

I had thought that was the end of it, yet here I was going back to research my roots once again. I just knew this time would be different. Over the phone, the woman I spoke to had told me there were files regarding my adoption, and that she would be glad to show them to me. She sounded young and friendly, so I hoped she would be helpful as well.

I didn't know if I was trembling because of my sickness, the cold breeze on my neck, or from nervousness. The nice lady had said she could tell me nothing over the phone; just that the files existed. She couldn't tell me if my biological parents were alive or dead, if they lived in Ohio, or in China or some other Asian country where the name "Wang" seemed to belong. I had so many questions: Was my birth illegitimate? What happened to my mother after giving me life and then giving me away? Did I have any brothers or sisters? If my mother still lived, would my re-emergence bring her sorrow or joy? What if I found my parents to be a type with whom I wouldn't want to associate? What if I discovered I had been conceived in an act of violence or as a result of incest?

I couldn't turn away now. I knew the information existed and I couldn't ignore it any longer. There was a strong possibility that both my birth parents were dead. They probably had not married and so the most I could hope for, if hope was the appropriate word, was the possibility of a half-sibling still living.

I turned up my collar, coughed to clear my throat, and walked into 100 East Eight with my friends Dianne and Joyce.

I had been right about the social worker. She was young and her smile was genuine. She introduced herself as Angela.

I took out a tape recorder and for a moment, her smile faltered. "Sorry," she said. "You can't use that. You can't make copies of the documents, either. It's just the rules."

I could tell she thought the rules were as nonsensical as they sounded. I thought of the old, stone-faced social worker I had met twenty years before. *She* probably wrote them!

Angela soon produced two slim folders. On one tab there was the faded name of "Grein," and on the other, "Wang." Joyce, my office manager, took out a pad and pen to take notes. Dianne sat beside me for moral support. Then, Angela began to read.

In summary, this is what I learned:

Dorothy Wang, my biological mother, had a relationship with a man named Robert Wilde, my biological father. He had worked seasonally on the Wang farm in Ohio, and he lived in a nearby community. Robert also worked at the Wright Aeronautical Corporation. Dorothy, then twenty-four, helped out maintaining the farm. The names of her parents, my grandparents, were Matthias and Lillian Wang.

All along I had assumed my birth parents lived far away, maybe even in Asia. Knowing they were from an area near my home town made my head spin.

In late December, 1941, Dorothy became pregnant. Robert, when

4

learning of the pregnancy in February 1942, suggested Dorothy take some "medication" that would abort the child. Dorothy refused, saying that such an action was sinful. Dorothy is listed in the report as "Roman Catholic," and Robert is listed as having no religion.

Once Dorothy refused the abortion, Robert seemed to offer minimal support. He drove her to appointments and paid the hospital bill, although there is no indication he visited the hospital or ever saw me, his child. Robert retained an attorney to handle the adoption procedure. The attorney visited Dorothy at home before the birth, and later in the hospital.

In March, 1942, Robert offered to marry Dorothy. His condition was that they be married by a Justice of the Peace. He wanted no part of a Catholic service. Dorothy declined his offer.

Dorothy delivered a baby boy on September 20, 1942. She did not name the child. Robert's attorney suggested that the baby not be brought to her room and that Dorothy should not visit the nursery. (This was a customary practice in the 1940's, to discourage bonding between the birth mother and her baby.)

The day after the delivery, Robert called Catholic Social Services and informed a social worker that Dorothy wished to release her baby for adoption. On September 25, the case worker visited Dorothy. In the social worker's report, she described Dorothy as a very strong girl who was used to outside farm work. She also noted a decided lisp. The social worker noted that Dorothy seemed disinterested in her baby and just wanted to sign whatever was required to finalize the adoption process. Dorothy said she would cooperate in whatever manner was necessary. When asked about the baby's father, she referred to a piece of paper from her purse with his name and address.

While in the hospital, Dorothy was visited by her parents. The report stated: "Her father, Matthias, has agreed that Dorothy may come home. Lillian, her mother, is anxious for Dorothy to return, as she needs her assistance in the home and on the farm."

Dorothy left the hospital without ever seeing the face of her child. At this point, Robert Wilde was dropped from the record.

Baby Wang, as I was called by the hospital staff, was transferred to the care of the Sisters of St. Joseph's Infant Home. On October 11, I was baptized Joseph Michael Wang.

Six months earlier, Catholic Social Services had accepted a formal application for adoption from Thelma and Frank Grein. A social worker did the usual background check and home investigation.

Thelma had been under a doctor's care since 1935 in an attempt to become pregnant, but her physician ultimately believed the couple would never be able to conceive a child.

Thelma was described as an attractive blonde who enjoyed taking care of children in the neighborhood. It was noted that Frank was rather shy. Frank said that he didn't care if the adopted child was a boy or girl, though he did add, "It would be nice to have a little boy to take bowling and to football and baseball games." It was noted that Frank's primary interests were his wife and his home. Frank was working as a roofer for his uncle, making $45 dollars a week, and it was possible that he could be drafted at any time. (America's involvement in World War II was picking up steam following the attack on Pearl Harbor on December 7, 1941.) The family received another $7.50 a week from Thelma's mother, Anna Kamphus, who worked in a local distillery and lived in the same house. Thelma stated that she felt lonely during the day, when both Frank and her mother were gone to work. She knew of several couples in the community who had adopted children through Catholic Social Services and hoped the process would work for her and Frank. She said she would prefer an infant under one year of age.

The report noted, "The home at 114 Moock Avenue has two bedrooms and a large yard. A child would, at first, stay in the room with the parents, as Mrs. Kamphus occupies the other bedroom. When the child grows larger, they would move to another home or expand the one they live in now."

The surrender of Joseph Michael Wang, (my name at the time) did not go without incident. Perhaps out of inattention, or perhaps because of second thoughts about the adoption, Dorothy Wang was delayed in giving up custody. On January 12, 1943, Catholic Social Services sent Dorothy the formal surrender papers. They needed her signature, (which she had been eager to give the day after the delivery) the signature of a witness, and the signed endorsement of a notary public.

By the beginning of February, Catholic Social Services had not yet received the papers. A social worker telephoned Dorothy, who said that because of inclement weather, her parents had not been able to drive her to the attorney's office, where the document could be notarized.

By the end of March, the surrender papers had still not been received. The social worker again called Dorothy, who said her father had been ill, but that they were going to see the attorney that evening. Finally, on April 2, the signed and notarized surrender papers were mailed to Catholic Social Services.

At the age of six months, I was finally placed in the home of Frank and Thelma Grein. After an introductory period of another six months, I could be adopted by the Greins.

Shortly after receiving their new child, Frank Grein was called up for military service.

On October 8, 1943, I was formally adopted by the Greins, and my name was legally changed to Roger Frank Grein.

The social worker reported, "He is such a happy baby, and they have fallen in love with him."

I cannot adequately describe my feelings as we walked out of the offices of the 100 East Eighth. The day was still gray and drizzly, the sounds and smells of the city were still the same, but I walked out with a new perspective. There was still much to learn, the first of which was whether my birth mother was still alive. Just having the names of my mother and father, having the outline of their story, and knowing that my mother had been a Catholic, was wonderful news. I might have been aborted, but my mother's faith had evidently saved me. My mind slowly processed these revelations. Despite the deluge of information, I felt myself thinking in a paced and orderly way. I suppose that was God's grace working within me.

I wondered if my mother had made the decision on her own, to give birth to me, and allow me to be adopted or if she had sought advice from others. Perhaps her faith was so strong that she knew what the right course should be. Was it her parents who helped her to decide? Was there another family member or friend involved in the decision-making? Were my grandparents loving, or did they consider the pregnancy a disgrace? How did Dorothy's siblings react? Were they ashamed of their sister or were they supportive?

I was certainly thankful for my mother's decision, but were there others to whom I should be thankful? I didn't know for sure, but I assumed there might be; and some of them might still be alive.

I was aware that during the 1940's, some parents disowned their unmarried pregnant daughters, but the record stated, "Dorothy may come home." Not only did my grandfather allow his daughter to return to his home, but he visited her in the hospital as well. I am only guessing, but I sense kindness and empathy by both parents. If this was indeed the case, then perhaps their love and support had ensured my survival; so, to them I owe an equal measure of gratitude.

Of one thing I was certain, Matthias and Lillian raised Dorothy in the Catholic faith. Dorothy had refused my biological father's wish for an abortion and a civil marriage. She had stated in the record that she believed abortion was "sinful." So, in addition to my mother and her family, I must give thanks to God and the Catholic Church for helping them discern their unerring course of action.

8

Strangely, for years I had had the premonition that abortion and I had met face to face. Now I knew that for a fact.

Through Dorothy's faith, God was watching over me. I was blessed. And then, when I was available for adoption, He was watching over me still, as I was blessed again with Frank and Thelma Grein as my adoptive parents.

All the time Angela had been reading the record of my early life, I felt a lump in my throat. It was only during the passage about the possibility of an abortion that I broke down and cried.

Upon learning that my mother's maiden name had been Wang, I drew all kinds of conclusions about my ancestry. Were my ancestors of Chinese or Eastern descent? My features certainly do not support such evidence, but who knows? I had lots of questions about this.

The kind social worker had read the reports precisely, with care and compassion. She understood the gravity of the moment. There was so much for me to absorb and so much significance to the dates of over half a century prior. I was startled to learn my grandparents were farmers. Had I not been adopted, I might very well have spent my life driving a tractor, rather than enjoying my more urban life among factories and busy city streets.

As the social worker read from the notes, she had given us directions to the Wang farm. "Take Springdale Road to Blue Rock...". That was all I needed to hear; I could find where my mother had lived! How exciting! Then she read that my father had worked at Wright Aeronautical Corporation. That was a stone's throw from my house in Lockland, and where my adoptive mother, Thelma, had worked during the war. Had they known one another?

I had been prepared to learn that my heritage may lay in other parts of the country, or other parts of the world. Now I was learning that my birth parents were never more than a half an hour away, and that my father had worked right around the corner from where I had grown up.

Next, I learned that I was born at the Good Samaritan Hospital. For years, I had presumed that a young woman had gone to the Infant Home midway through her pregnancy, given birth there, and stayed with me until I was adopted. I had envisioned it all wrong!

9

Dorothy entered the hospital September 20 and was discharged September 29, 1942. In all that time, she never saw my face. I was startled. How could she not have held me and given me a mother's blessing? After a bit of reflection, it became obvious to me that my mother loved me. Dorothy had fought to prevent an abortion. If my mother cared that much for me before I was born, I couldn't doubt her love after my birth. Rather than feeling hurt, I felt great sorrow for my mother.

I had to decide. Should I look for her now? Should I look for my father? Should I tell him I forgive him for wanting to have me killed? If I am successful in my search for them, will I bring tragedy to their current families? I might unleash old hurts long since put to rest. Will this be a selfish quest?

On the other hand, there were things I deserved to know. Were there family medical illnesses that lurked unbeknownst to me? Was Dorothy's reported lisp a genetic connection to my own disability?

The report had said that my mother was "mentally slow." Is that why I had to study so much harder than my classmates? What would Dorothy think of my Master's Degree? Did my mother's disability contribute to her involvement in a sexual indiscretion? Was she raped?

The more I learned, the more I wanted to know.

What struck me the most was the timing; it was as if God had been orchestrating my whole life. What would have happened if the Greins had adopted their baby from another agency, or had not submitted the adoption application to Catholic Social Services? What would have happened if Dorothy had returned the adoption papers immediately, rather than three months late? What would have happened if the officials at the hospital or the Infant Home had noticed my disability? Any of these factors could have changed the trajectory of my life.

What I *do* know is that I owe my very life to Dorothy Wang, and to Frank and Thelma Grein. When I left the office building, and walked out into the humid air on that drizzly morning, I took a deep breath and thanked God for those three people.

CHAPTER 2

"WHY DO YOU WALK FUNNY?"

I was sixty-five years old before I had a name for my disability: cerebral palsy. Before that, I was known as the boy who walked funny.

When a Sister from the orphanage called the Grein residence on April 13, 1943, she said, "You can pick up your son anytime." My parents scrambled quickly for furniture and baby clothes suitable for a sixth-month-old boy. The neighbor behind their house gave them a crib. Another neighbor, around the corner, gave them baby clothes and diapers. By that night I was in their home. My new parents stayed up late that night, just looking at me, even when I was sleeping. To them, it was as if I had just been born.

The town I came to live in that day sat on the edge of the Miami-Erie Canal; a massive ditch built in 1825 between Cincinnati and Toledo, to connect the water traffic of the Mississippi and Ohio Rivers with the commerce of the Great Lakes. Just blocks away from our home sat a flood lock to regulate water levels in the canal. It is from this lock that our town got its name: Lockland.

In 1943, Lockland was a factory town and within its municipal limits of one square mile, over 5,000 people were employed in gigantic brick-walled factories turning out everything from mattresses to cardboard boxes. To the south was Cincinnati and to the east, Reading, a German Catholic blue-collar town where my parents had spent their childhoods.

My new home was located at 114 Moock Avenue. Just as it was near to the canal, so too our house was near everything else. Mill Street, the main street of the town, was just a few minutes' walk away, and a grocery store was just around the corner. Our street was quiet, lined with oak trees and modest wood and brick homes.

A painting of the house I lived in for 75 years.

At the time of my adoption, World War II was at full throttle. Soon after I was taken to my new home, Dad was sent to California for the Army's basic training. He later went to Europe to fight in the Battle of the Bulge. Mother went to work second shift at Wright Aeronautical, making war materials. A neighbor would come over, while Mom worked, to care for me until Grandma Kamphus got off work at the National Distillery.

Grandma's husband had deserted his family years before, leaving my mother, Thelma Kamphus, and her sister, without a father in the home. The small family moved to Reading, Ohio, where there were relatives nearby. While Grandma worked in the distillery, her two girls dropped out of school as soon as they were old enough. To earn extra money, they cleaned houses and babysat. My mother used to tell me how she would walk along the railroad tracks near their house, collecting bits of coal that had fallen from the trains. This was their fuel for heating and cooking.

Frank Grein's family had also struggled. During the early years of the Great Depression, Dad's father worked as a carpenter and then as a security guard in Reading. Although the family avoided the bread lines, times were lean. There were six children to feed. When he was old enough, my adoptive dad went to work for the Civilian Conservation Core. (The CCC was a program initiated in 1933 to help pull our country out of the Great Depression. It provided conservation work for unemployed young men in urban areas. In Cincinnati, that meant building a retaining wall near the Ohio River.)

I don't know how Mother and Dad met, but I'm sure it must have started with a casual introduction, probably at a church function. They were married September 5, 1934, during a weekday Mass. Because it was a school day, the church grounds were overrun with children. My mother loved children and was probably thinking of their offspring to come.

Wedding Photo of my parents

After the ceremony, Mother and Dad went back to the Grein household for breakfast. Then they borrowed a Model-T car and went to the Indiana State Fair. They came back the same day. That was their honeymoon - Depression style.

About this time, Dad was working for his uncle at a roofing and tin shop in Reading. Mom settled into their home on Moock Avenue and prepared to start a family.

I sometimes try to envision my mom during those years, wanting to have children so badly, and yet, year after year, not being able to have a child of her own. Her job was to be a supportive wife and maintain a home. All around her, she watched neighborhood kids play and couples walk with their strollers. It surely was a sad and lonely time for her.

As for Dad, I have a harder time imagining what he was going through. Dad was quiet, prudent, and a hard worker. He believed love should be shown with actions and hard labor rather than with words. I know he must have been disappointed with their inability to conceive a child. I'm sure too, that seeing my mother's pain could not have been easy for him to bear. They probably didn't share these deep feelings of emptiness with each other. They were stoic Germans, after all!

So, when the call came from the Infant Home, eight years of longing must have quickly melted away. Mother was 29 and Dad 31 at the time I came to live with them.

When Father left for the war, shortly after my arrival, my world was Mother, my babysitter, Roberta, and Grandma Kamphus. Roberta has since told me that I was the joy of my mother's life. Thelma, my mom, would dress me up in the best clothes she could afford, was always singing to me, and would show me off at every opportunity.

Mom with me

But when it came time for me to walk, there was a problem. I positioned my feet differently than other toddlers, and could not keep my balance. I would skip a few steps on my toes and then fall over.

It wasn't that noticeable at first. Not having raised another child before me, my mother probably thought it was just part of normal development. But at some point, doubt crept into her mind. I wasn't getting any better and others began to notice my struggles.

On June 2, 1944, my mom made a call to a woman at the Infant Home. Mom told her that I was beginning to walk, but was walking on my toes in a peculiar fashion. She was referred to Catholic Social Services, which she telephoned immediately.

On June 5, Mother took me to the doctor in our neighborhood when I was three months shy of my second birthday. She sat in quiet shock as a birth injury was diagnosed. The doctor told her that I might never walk, talk or even know her. She managed what questions she could. "Will this show up in other ways?" "Perhaps," was all the doctor would tell her. "Is there anything I can do to help my baby walk better?" she asked. Again, there was the reply, "Perhaps." He instructed her to regularly stretch my legs and massage my muscles. The doctor told her that I might walk and talk someday, but my behavior and abilities would be different from other children. He couldn't assure her at that time that I would not be affected mentally. There had been no indication of a birth defect at the hospital, nor had there been any indication of distress at the Infant Home. There was one notation about a slight tremor in my right arm shortly following my birth, and another note by the Infant Home that said, "His sitting behavior has always lagged behind other areas of development. Baby Wang has an attractive personality and a seemingly even disposition. He may be considered suitable for adoption."

From then on, every day, Mother massaged my feet. She took me out to walk, instructing my every step with, "Heel-toe, heel-toe, heel-toe," to keep me from walking on my toes, which was my natural inclination. She wrote to Dad about my disability, trying not to show her disappointment. He was stationed in California at that time, but soon left to fight in Europe. Mom was all on her own.

After waiting so many years, the only child she would ever have was disabled!

"Take him back," said one family member. But my mother loved me and she was used to struggle. She would not give up on me, and she would not "trade me in" for another child.

When anyone suggested that I be "taken back," Mother would say, "Well, I love his pretty blue eyes." I knew she was disappointed; who wouldn't be? But she accepted me for who I was, and then worked tirelessly to raise me in the best way she knew. She had to go through all of this alone, as Dad was stationed far away.

In addition to an irregular gait, I also slurred my speech, and my sense of balance was shaky. But in my earliest memories, I don't recall being aware of any difference between me and the rest of the children with whom I played.

In 1946, Dad was honorably discharged and came home. Grandma Kamphus moved out, and Mother quit work to stay home with me. From then on, wherever she went, I was in tow; to the butcher, the bakery, and errands on Mill street. We were always together.

It was about this time that Mother and Dad told me I had been adopted. They told me as soon as they felt I could grasp the concept.

They did it well, and the news was not a blow; actually, it made me feel very special. That feeling has never left me.

As time passed, my playing with the neighborhood kids became more earnest and independent of Mother. When my friends and I got to be five years old, we were allowed to leave the yard. The gravel service lane behind my house became our playground.

Soon, my friends were riding bicycles on the sidewalks. It took me a while to learn to ride a bike because of my disability, but I kept trying. To mount the bike, I would stand on an upside-down wash tub and then push off. Often I would fall on my face, and one time I busted my knee so badly I had to go to the hospital. But, I didn't give up, and finally I learned to ride a bike.

There were other activities that challenged me at first, but I eventually overcame them. An example of one skill that came easily to my friends was climbing an old cherry tree in our backyard. I sat, watched and waited, until everyone was called home. Then, slowly and methodically, I managed to climb that tree. I imagine Mother watched anxiously from the kitchen window, as she let me do it alone.

The slow and methodical approach would stay with me the rest of my life. It wasn't so much a matter of choosing to do things that way; it was the ONLY way I could do them.

At age five, I went to Kindergarten. All my neighborhood friends were there, and it was a wonderful time. I did normal little boy things, too, that were both an aggravation and a source of endearment for my parents. I let a relative's chickens loose once; another time, I locked myself in the bathroom and had to be pulled from the window by the fire department.

My first and second grades were challenging. I remember peeing on the floor because I was too shy to raise my hand. I was not doing well in my studies, either. Reading was especially difficult, so Mother took me to a tutor in the summer.

During those first six years of my life, God was truly protecting me. Even before I was aware, He was watching over me. Some might say I had an unfortunate childhood because I never knew my real mother and father, I was given up for adoption, and I suffered a birth injury that would forever leave me disabled. But I didn't look at it that way.

First, rather than aborting me, a scared young woman decided to bring me into the world, with whatever humiliation and lost opportunity that decision might have cost her. Then, through the work of the Sisters at the Infant Home, God choose my loving adoptive parents. They were wonderful people who, through their own struggles, showed me how to persevere and overcome obstacles. God gave me something else, too. He gave me, even as a young boy, the ability to feel good about myself. That was no small feat for a child who, when encountering a potential playmate, was first asked, "Why do you walk funny?"

CHAPTER 3

THE YOUNG ENTREPRENEUR

For as long as I can remember, I have been an entrepreneur. When an addition to the school was being built around the corner from our house in 1948, I hung around until after the workers left, then I would pick up their discarded pop and beer bottles. The grocer, a few doors from my house, gave me two cents for each pop bottle and a nickel for each beer bottle. I usually made one or two dollars each day. That was a *fortune* for a six-year-old child back then.

By the time I was seven, I had saved enough money to buy a Radio Flyer red wagon, which I used to go up and down the street, knocking on doors and collecting old newspapers the neighbors would save for me. A salvage company in town paid me by the pound.

Looking back, my youthful money-making enterprises were solitary activities. Perhaps my playmates didn't want to leave their sports games to earn a few coins. Perhaps I didn't want to include them, for fear of having to share my profits. Maybe, on a subconscious level, I was tired of trying to keep up with them in sports. Regardless of my motivations, once I saw the rewards of my entrepreneurial efforts, I was hooked.

I was about nine years old in this photo.

By the time I was ten, I was cutting lawns with a push mower I had purchased with my newspaper and bottle collecting money. At twelve, I was cutting eight lawns a week and had graduated to a motor-driven mower. Eventually I bought two more mowers, so I could always have one working while the other two were being serviced. I was known as "The Mower Boy" in my neighborhood over the next ten years. In the autumn I raked leaves and in the winter, I shoveled snow. Year-round, I delivered papers for two newspapers: one each morning, and one each afternoon. Years later, the mayor of Lockland joked with me that, due to my industriousness, I could have been supporting myself even then!

I certainly did have more money than most young boys. What did I do with it? When I was nine, I joined the Christmas Club at our local bank, and thus was able to buy presents for my parents. Being able to reciprocate my parents' love in a tangible and grown-up way excited me tremendously. I don't recall what I bought, but the act of unselfish giving served as a real rite of passage for me.

My mother supported me in all of these activities. She took me to buy the wagon, she helped me haul my collection of newspapers to the salvage company in the trunk of her car, and she co-signed for my first savings account.

It wasn't until much later that I learned my parents, though always expressing confidence in me, were terribly concerned about my future. No one knew if my physical condition might worsen, and if so, whether I would be able to take care of myself as an adult.

Perhaps this concern gave them extra impetus to make sure I was not only encouraged to excel at activities of my own interest, but I was also given the opportunity to participate in almost every other pursuit in which boys of that time were engaged.

I played knothole baseball, and I took accordion and trombone lessons. I even took tap-dancing classes, because Mother thought it might help me with my walking. I attended religious education on Saturday mornings, and participated in the Boy Scouts. I was also awarded a position on the safety patrol of my school.

By sixth grade, I began to go to birthday and Halloween parties with my friends. These often turned into "kissing parties," where we would play "spin-the-bottle" or "Post Office" with the neighborhood girls. Mothers were upstairs or in another room and not present. Sixth grade was a wonderful time to be alive!

In the seventh grade I was voted Vice President of the class. I was part of the "in-crowd." It was another memorable year in my life.

By the time I was in the ninth grade, I was mowing up to thirty yards a week; sometimes as many as eleven per day, if we had experienced a lot of rain. Just as my mowing business was increasing, so were the leaf raking and snow shoveling jobs.

In the winter, I was often awake by 5:00 a.m. and soon thereafter, in somebody's driveway pitching snow. I got paid by the job, so if the snow had been light, I could do a lot of drives and sidewalks, and make a lot of money quickly. If the snow had been heavy, the customer got a deal.

I was about fourteen in this photo.

I liked leaf raking the least. I got paid by the hour, so I couldn't increase the number of hours available, and I could never increase my income, no matter how efficiently I worked.

In my free time, I also helped my dad by cutting shingles and cleaning up after his roofing jobs.

It wasn't until I was sixteen that, purely by happenstance, I got a glimpse into entrepreneurship on a higher level. I was curious about a hotel being built in Reading. The whole idea of it intrigued me: the construction, the people who would pay to stay there, and the investors who would be putting up the money to build it. A light bulb went on in my mind. I realized that to be truly financially successful, I couldn't just count on the number of hours I could fill with my own labor. There was something else at work here, and I wanted to be a part of it.

I began asking questions of the town's mayor, my high school principal and the school superintendent. How could investors have that much money? How did they accrue it? Can I do the same? Each of these men was generous with his time mentoring me. Slowly, and with great patience, they introduced me to the concept of investment.

It may seem strange today, that I would have such easy access to people of such standing; but remember, the town of Lockland was very small - only one square mile. It enjoyed the blessings and disadvantages of everyone knowing everyone else. The school superintendent lived across the street from me. The principal lived around the corner, and the mayor was about five blocks away. When I wasn't cutting their lawns, they saw me in school. The mayor was my history teacher.

These men, and several others, gathered regularly to participate in an investment club. Aware of my interest, they invited me to join them. They also suggested I take an evening class about stocks and bonds at Norwood High School.

When I completed the evening class, several members of the club drove me to downtown Cincinnati, to introduce me to a stock broker. I was seventeen at the time. After that visit, my history teacher excused me from class if I needed to call my stockbroker. Years later he told me that I was the only kid he knew who left class early to make money.

My high school class of 1961 had one hundred and ten students enrolled in our freshman year; but only fifty-three of us made it to graduation. We prepared for a celebratory trip to Washington D.C. and Gettysburg. For years we had been raising money for this trip. We sold magazines, Easter eggs, raffle tickets and whatever else that would get us a little closer to our goal. I always sold the most, won the prizes and set the pace for my classmates. It just came naturally. I worked at fundraising as I had with the yard work: continuously.

We ended up taking a bus and spending a week together. The things we saw and the fun we had made that time very special! I hold those memories dear. We had worked so hard, seen each other grow up, and had been good friends for many years. We returned on a Saturday morning, and then, true to my work ethic, I cut grass for eleven yards!

I wonder what my parents must have thought about all of my interest in investing. Though I sensed their approval, they never said anything about it. Perhaps they just saw me filling my time with work, as they had always done. I really didn't have a lot of time for other tasks or interests, and we never discussed it.

CHAPTER 4

THE YOUNG SPORTS ENTHUSIAST

It wasn't until I was old enough for organized sports that the repercussions of my disability really began to sink in. Up until then I had suffered the humiliation of always being chosen last for the teams. But lots of kids get chosen last, and I still got to play. After many times of being the last one picked, however, I shifted my way of thinking. Rather than dreading the shame, I just hoped I would end up on the better team.

When it came time for organized sports in the seventh grade, things changed. The first and only sport I tried out for was basketball. While the other boys raced from net to net, I was stuck at center court, running a few steps this way and then that, utterly unable to keep up. Having played with the same kids over the years, I now suddenly found my name excluded from the team roster. I was cut. What bothered me so much was the fact that I was the ONLY one from among my friends who did not make the team. Worse yet, I was taller than any other boy of my age!

I had always found a way to participate before, and now I could not. I had to watch from the bleachers. It was this one incident that made me come to terms with the fact that I was different from the other kids.

There are few things more heart-wrenching than a child being told, in one fashion or another, that he doesn't belong; that he is worthless because of a physical limitation beyond his control. I came home and cried like a baby. It was an event so earth-shattering that it still moves me to this day.

I often wonder how much my parents grieved for me that evening. In the small world of Lockland, surely they would have learned about my painful rejection, even if I didn't tell them. They must have concluded that their son had finally had to face what they had dreaded for years: the acknowledgement that I was different from the other children, and this difference would stay with me for the duration of my life. I can imagine them quietly agonizing over it after I had gone to bed that night.

In conversation with others, I cannot detect that my voice is slurred, except occasionally when a look of confusion appears on the listener's face. Likewise, if I am walking down a street, my gait seems to me to be the same as that of anyone else. Today, I view this non-recognition as a blessing. As a kid, it took isolated incidents, such as the anguish of trying out for the basketball team, to drive the message home to me: "There really are some things you can't do, Roger."

Just as I was feeling cut off from my small world, God seemed to send an angel to my rescue. The day after the basketball tryouts, the coach called me into his office. He asked if I would be interested in managing the team with him. I jumped at the opportunity. It meant hauling water, picking up towels drenched with sweat, and doing other drudge work, but the important thing was, I was back with my friends. Some might see this as an insignificant event. The coach needed an assistant manager and perhaps he felt I was the only one who would take the job. To me, his was a gesture of immense importance. It allowed me to accept my limitations and to move forward. It allowed me to be part of the team after all!

This position continued throughout my seventh and eighth grades. Beginning in the ninth grade, I was assistant manager for the football, basketball and baseball teams. Though I continued to be disappointed I couldn't play, I was still happy to be a valuable member of the teams. In all of the team photos each year, I proudly stood up with my friends.

I'm in the last row far left.

Like our coach, other adults and teachers in my life sometimes took a special interest in me, giving me the benefit of the doubt, giving me extra opportunities, and pushing me to be the best young man I could be. But they would also give me a failing grade if I deserved it!

CHAPTER 5

FAMILY LIFE

During these years of emerging interests and self-knowledge, life with my family was simple and loving. I believe that everyone took an interest in giving me a happy childhood.

I grew up in a Catholic German household. Cincinnati was one of the most German cities in the United States as well as one of the most conservative. Mark Twain once remarked, "When the end of the world comes, I want to be in Cincinnati. Everything that happens comes there ten years later than anywhere else!"

My family ate fish and macaroni on Fridays; my mother wore a veil to Mass each Sunday; the nuns still wore their habits; and I studied the Baltimore Catechism. My formative years were of another era. We didn't question our faith. We were told what to believe and how to behave.

The word of my parents was law. They followed a very scripted code of behavior, one formed out of an ancestral Germanic stoicism, and the more recent tribulations of the Great Depression and World War II. Providing food for our table and a roof over my head were the ways they expressed their love for me. My father and mother never hugged or kissed me, nor did I expect or want them to.

I came to know the sincere and unconditional love of Christ and of my parents. It was all very simple. It was all I needed.

My parents also believed in authority. It was President Franklin Roosevelt's "New Deal" that had provided a job for my dad and members of our community. It was the strong central government that had saved their very way of life during WWII. My Dad, in particular, reflected the characteristics of his Depression-era generation. Until late in life, he never challenged authority. He wanted just the facts, and if there weren't facts to talk about, such as a baseball score or a roofing job, he just kept quiet. At the dinner table, he did little but eat.

My mother, on the other hand, talked a lot. She liked to converse on the phone and on the porch swing with friends. Mom discussed her opinion of all manner of things. However, I never really learned about her hopes, aspirations and disappointments she may have had, and I regret not asking her about those things as she reached the end of her life.

I have always possessed a relentless drive to obtain goals. This compulsiveness to act upon my desires has also played a role in my relationship with the Catholic Church.

Early in my schooling, the nuns drilled into me that the goal of life is to love and serve God and my fellow man in order to enter into eternal happiness with God in heaven. I took these lessons seriously, and I craved Christ's love for no other reason than its very goodness. His love made sense of my world. It was His love that gave my biological mother, Dorothy, the courage to deliver me and then let me go. It was His love that had enabled Thelma Grein to work through the trauma of my disability and teach me to do likewise. I owed Him.

Once or twice each summer, Mother would get together with her friends and take a throng of kids to an amusement park, sometimes riding a large boat up the Ohio River to get there. On other occasions she would take us to the Cincinnati Zoo. Grandma Kamphus loved to go to church festivals on summer weekends, so with me in tow, she would buy us Sunday passes for the city bus to travel to the festivals all over Cincinnati. Each summer I spent a week or two with my father's parents in Reading. Occasionally, I would go to a Cincinnati Reds' game with my dad.

Sometimes Mom, Dad and I would take a short vacation during the spring and winter when Dad's roofing workload was lighter. We went to Virginia Beach, Florida, the Great Smokey Mountains National Park and Mammoth Cave.

My trip to Florida with Mom and Dad in 1963

By far, the biggest vacation we ever undertook was traveling to the Rose Bowl and Disneyland over the 1957-58 New Year. We rode the train to Chicago and then boarded another sight-seeing train to California. I was filled with awe, watching the amazing landscapes of the American West roll past my window. When I think of my mother riding these luxury trains, I wonder if she recalled the many times as a youngster she used to follow the coal trains, hoping to collect spilled pieces of fuel to heat their home.

Disneyland was, of course, great for me. It was the first year the park was open and I was enamored with all of it. Then there was the Rose Bowl parade. To cap things off, we watched Ohio State beat Oregon 10-7 in the Rose Bowl game with a fourth quarter field goal. Dad was ecstatic! I will never forget that California trip. In a way, it was the honeymoon my parents never had.

The once weekly activity I relished the most was akin to just enjoying life. Such were the visits each Sunday evening to Dad's parents. We would arrive around 7:30 p.m. to watch the Ed Sullivan show and then play cards until 11:00. Sometimes, at our house, after we had purchased a television, we would invite neighbors over to watch the big Saturday evening wrestling shows. Other times I would just lie on the floor and listen to Amos and Andy on the radio. When I say my parents made a good life for me, these family activities and events are some of the things that I recall with great affection.

I'm in the striped shirt on the floor. Mom and Dad are seated behind me.
Aunt Bernie and her two children and Grandma Kamphus are also with us.

When I turned sixteen, the excitement of driver's education and the prospect of having a car, and real freedom, was exhilarating. My coach was my driving instructor. We rode with three other students in the car. I remember one of the students would cruelly mimic my disability. The coach let this behavior go on for about a month before putting a stop to it. He told me later that I had to learn a way to deal with such ridicule, because as an adult, I wouldn't have him around to protect me.

One thing Coach didn't know was that the head neurologist in Cincinnati had advised my mother that I should never drive. With my mother and me seated before his desk, he told us frankly that my brain had "short fuses" that might not be able to handle the stress of driving. At that, Mother blew her fuse, and then otherwise ignored him. She was determined to prove him wrong, and from then on put me in the driver's seat at every opportunity. She knew, more than I did, how important driving would be in my life as an independent adult.

Reflecting on these days of my youth, I recognize how my home life was different than that of children growing up today. As a boy, I was happy and in want of nothing. Even as an adolescent and young adult, I never felt I was missing out on anything.

When I look back on those school years I am amazed by the outpouring of care and concern that my neighbors, coaches and teachers afforded me. The principal's note to the teachers at the time sums it up: "Always try to make the child be tall inside." They certainly did that for me.

I sometimes wonder if my biological mother was thinking about me during those years. Was she sorry she gave me away? I think she would have been content to know that I was being supported by a loving family and community.

CHAPTER 6

FIRST CRUSH

While some of my friends were starting to be paired with a member of the opposite sex, and going steady, I had only the occasional date. In fact, I could never quite join the dating scene. Despite my successful boyhood businesses, I lacked self-confidence when it came to girls. I could sit and talk to adults all day and not be intimidated in the least, but to pick up the phone with the idea of asking a girl out was a whole other ball game. I knew others could do it, but not me.

I would get together with other guys who didn't date, or at least didn't date often. We would go bowling, to ball games or to the neighborhood swimming pool. I missed not having a girlfriend. Like a lot of guys, I surmised that a close friendship with a female confidant would make me feel whole. I believed a relationship with a girl would be the answer to everything.

When I was sixteen, my attention was drawn to a new kid in the neighborhood. She was only twelve at that time. I don't recall the first time I saw her, but I do remember that whenever and however I first became aware of her, I was smitten.

In my mind, she was an angel with a smile like I had never seen. If God ever created the perfect face, he had done it with her. I'll call her Carol for purposes of anonymity.

Growing up, I had my share of puppy loves and little sweethearts. I had played the silly kissing games at birthday parties, held a few hands at the movie theater, but nothing had prepared me for Carol. When you are older, love is a decision; when are young, it's just a matter of what makes your heart pound. My heart pounded for Carol.

At first we got to know each other with little snippets of "Hi!" and "How are you doing?" I don't know how I introduced myself, but before long we were having longer conversations about school and sports. She was very pleasant and kind, and always receptive to our little conversations.

I could not, however, figure a way around the age difference that separated us. I knew when I graduated from high school, she would just be entering as a Freshman. We lived in different worlds. I was not ashamed of my feelings for her, but I was aware of others' possible perceptions. I knew Carol's parents would not like me calling, because Carol was too young to go out with me. So, I waited, biding my time, remaining discreet and trying to stay in her good graces.

By the time she was fourteen, she was maturing in very obvious ways, and my heart pounded even faster. She touched me to my teenage core; and with all my heart I wanted to share my life with her.

Despite my unrequited obsession, I still had brief moments of clear thinking. I wondered if in my secret devotion to Carol, I was missing out on other relationships with girls closer to my age. I got up the nerve to call a few of them to ask out on dates. We did go and had a good time. But despite dating others, the image of Carol would sneak up in my mind, totally against my will.

CHAPTER 7

THE COLLEGE EXPERIENCE

College was by no means a sure thing for me. My high school grades were mediocre, and though I was not totally aware of it, my disability hung over me like a dark cloud. Even my mother and father had their doubts about my chances for success in higher education. Years later, our family doctor revealed to me conversations he had had with my mother, who would confide her anxieties to him. She was concerned that my condition would prevent me from attending college and from supporting myself as an adult. At that time, so little was known about the source and course of cerebral palsy. No one could predict if it would worsen or how it might manifest itself under certain conditions. It was only normal for my mother to have doubts about my future, but up until that time, I could probably count on one hand how many times thoughts of my disability kept me awake at night. I'm sure those nights were much more numerous for my parents.

I've discovered that God places "angels" in our path at just the right time: people who intervene in a blessed way and to such a degree that one's whole life changes course, or perhaps returns to the course God had intended all along. Our family doctor was one such "angel."

His curiosity about my condition and his love for me allowed him to overlook my slurred speech, my irregular gait, and my spastic behavior. It was as though he was staring into a pool of disturbed water, trying to perceive the bottom. What he saw, he told my mother, was a boy whose mental capacity was the same as any ordinary youngster not affected by cerebral palsy. College and a successful career were within my abilities. He said this not just once, but over and over. Our doctor took a studied interest in my future.

On another level, I'm sure my parents were looking at college with a very practical eye. My father worked extremely hard, but our lifestyle was modest. College tuition would be a stretch. Would it be worth the investment? Would this money be spent in a cause that would, in the end, be futile? Our family doctor said, "NO!"

About this time, I attended a college fair held at Lockland High School. One of the ladies there represented the Ohio Department of Vocational Rehabilitation. After some conversation with her, she told me I might be eligible for a tuition scholarship. For once, my disability would be working in my favor! My parents were elated.

I began looking in earnest for a college to attend. I had decided on a career goal as a stockbroker. There were only three universities near Cincinnati with this major to be considered, because I did not want to move far away: Miami University at Oxford, Xavier University and the University of Cincinnati (U.C.).

In our senior year at Lockland High School, a friend and I visited Oxford. It was too far from home to commute, and so I would have had to live on campus. I was not ready for dorm life. Xavier University, on the other hand, was the closest one to Lockland, but I considered it too "brainy" for me. Even with the Vocational Rehab scholarship, the tuition would have been more than my parents' savings and my grass cutting proceeds could have handled.

That left U.C. There were several things going for that school. First, it was close enough that I could continue living at home. Second, several of my Lockland classmates had already been accepted there. Lastly, and perhaps most significantly, they had a collegiate basketball team which was a perennial power at the national level. Oscar Robertson was playing at that time! I went to U.C.

My high school graduation photo

Because I had always attended summer school at Lockland, and perhaps because I felt I had something to prove, I decided to apply for admission to U.C. for the summer session immediately following high school graduation. This was not the usual course for most students who liked to take the summer off. I had an interview with an admissions official and we talked for a long while. He had my records, which he thumbed through occasionally. Mostly, though, we talked about my businesses, my interest in the stock market, and my high school experiences managing the sports teams. It was a comfortable conversation without most of the questions I had anticipated. Shortly thereafter, I got a letter of acceptance. Its arrival was a banner day for my parents.

It was only later, when I counted the admissions officer among my friends, that I learned my mediocre grades in high school were not nearly good enough to qualify for entrance. Had I applied for fall admission, as did the majority of entering freshmen, I would not have been accepted. He explained that it was my extracurricular activities that swung the decision in favor of my admission. Had I decided to enter in the fall, rather than in the summer, I would not have had an interview, and the extent of my activities would not have been evident. Again, God placed another "angel" in my path, and this blessing made all the difference in my future successes.

I didn't know what had influenced his decision to accept me at that time, but I did recognize that this was an opportunity to seize. A basic change occurred in my attitude toward studying. I buckled down and declined any unnecessary activities. I chose to major in finance and minor in accounting, still with the career goal of stockbroker. I felt drawn to the work. The stacks of ledgers under my bed, reflecting everything from the customer whose grass needed cutting when, to how much a particular customer had paid me, attested to my interest in numbers and record-keeping. My natural youthful interests were at last finding a higher expression that could take me places worthwhile and exciting. It was my ticket to successful adulthood.

Some classes were a struggle, such as English and calculus, but my business classes more than made up for those I did not enjoy. Anything having to do with economics, investments and accounting was a pleasure. I particularly enjoyed Principles of Accounting, taught by a gentleman who would later play a much larger role in my life. It was my time to thrive!

On the social scene, several of my buddies from Lockland were with me at U.C. We made a point of going to basketball games together. In 1961 and 1962, the U.C. team won the national championship. In 1963 we lost to Loyola of Chicago in overtime in the championship game. I was there. I went to all the games. I would stand for hours for tickets and would arrive hours early to get the best seat in the student section. It was a thrilling experience.

And then there was the Cincinnati Reds baseball team, which went to the World Series in 1961. Cincinnati seemed to be at the center of the world that year!

College also expanded my universe of possible relationships with the opposite sex. It seemed every direction I looked there was someone of interest. But, again, I lacked the self-confidence to ask anyone out. I still wasn't over Carol.

When I had graduated from high school, it wasn't lost on me that

Carol was graduating from the eight grade. Now, I thought, she would be old enough to go out. If I were going to start a relationship with her, this might be my last chance. I decided to call her for the first time and ask her to a Reds' baseball game. I wrote down what I was going to say and what things we could talk about. I finally worked up the nerve and made the call.

"No," Carol said. She couldn't go to the Reds game with me. Her parents wouldn't let her. She was too young, they said. Her words crushed me. I made as graceful an exit as I could and hung up. "Well, then," I thought, "That's the end of it."

But, of course, it wasn't the end. I still thought about her. I thought about her on those few occasions in college when I was out with other girls. I still thought she was "the one."

Carol had by no means given me the cold shoulder. She wasn't allowed to date yet, that's all. She had shown me the same warmth and the same willingness to share her time with me that she had always done.

So, in my second year of college, I asked her out again. This time she didn't have to ask her parents. She said, "Yes." Finally, I thought, this beautiful girl will be on my arm.

Carol and I went out twice that year; both times to Red's baseball games. I enjoyed her company, and was somewhat in awe of her presence. I was still distracted by that wonderful smile. I couldn't believe it was actually Carol sitting there waiting for me, as I was coming down the steps with hot dogs and cokes. Sports were so important to me, and a good Red's game was truly one of life's pleasures, *and* I had Carol to enjoy it with, finally!

But even as we enjoyed our time together, I was able to see that nothing was clicking between us. The spontaneity wasn't there. The easy laughter was missing. We had a good time, but the Earth didn't move for her or for me.

It was an awakening, really. Carol had changed and I had changed. I had moved on in ways indiscernible even to myself. It was both a disappointment and a relief.

It wasn't long after our second date that Carol began seeing a

Lockland boy her own age. I still had enough hangover from the old feelings to be hurt, but I wasn't devastated. Several years later I heard she was marrying the same boy. My feelings for her resurfaced, but I was ready to let her go. Her marriage gave my mind an excuse for a clean separation. I still think of her from time to time, and treasure the memory.

It was a sweet, innocent time for us both. And, man, what a smile!

CHAPTER 8
THE JOB MARKET

I graduated from the University of Cincinnati with a Bachelor's Degree in Business Administration. Just prior to graduation, the headhunters descended for the harvest of promising young graduates. Like my friends, I was eager to begin a career. I signed up for as many interviews as I could; mostly in the accounting field. I had given up the idea of being a stockbroker. In those days you needed to be from the "right" family, and to travel with the inner circles of Cincinnati's high society. I did not have the pedigree required.

Although all of the interviewers were very kind and seemed genuinely interested in me, I soon noticed I was not getting the same outcomes as my peers, who were flying around the country for second interviews. I was putting my all into it, but was repeatedly rejected or ignored. It was my disability, the "extra baggage" that was my obstacle. Ever since I could remember, it took weeks, if not months, for me to impress upon friends, teachers and coaches that the disability did not factor in what I could accomplish. How could I relay that fact in a forty-five-minute job interview? I couldn't! I got one second interview in Chicago, which didn't amount to anything.

Was I bitter? Maybe a little. I recognized that I didn't really want to leave the Cincinnati area. Had the Chicago job materialized, it would have been a traumatizing experience. For whatever reason, staying close to home has always given me a great deal of security. I like to visit other places, but I always want to return to Cincinnati and my home in Lockland. I noted the general rejection of the interview experiences, but it was only later that its significance really sank in.

Upon my graduation, aware that I was unemployed, the manager of the Lockland office of the First National Bank asked if I would be interested in working at the bank's headquarters in downtown Cincinnati. I said I would, and with his recommendation, I landed a job in the trust department. I reported to the tax division and was responsible for the tax returns of bank clients. The pay was $75 per week; this was about half of what my fellow graduates were making and what I had anticipated making. But I didn't complain. I was led to believe there was a possibility of promotion within the bank over time, and besides, I was happy to be working in Cincinnati.

In my last year in college, I began attending the Neumann Club activities. This was an organization for Catholic students. When I began working for the bank, I attended Mass during my lunch hour each day. The lack of wholeness that I had thought only a woman could fill, was now being more than compensated through my relationship with God.

I continued praying the Rosary each morning, going to daily Mass, and I prayed on my knees each night. I confessed my sins regularly and observed each Holy Day. I wanted to be in touch with Christ every minute of every day, and to respond to each challenge according to His Holy Will. By walking with Christ, I felt a touch of His insight, His patience and His wisdom. Without God, there would be no meaning in my life.

Frank and Thelma had always impressed upon me that when reaching adulthood, each person is free to make his own decisions in life. My parents taught me that faith is personal and that, just as I appreciated the opportunity to worship as I chose, so too the beliefs of others must be respected. I learned that it is not my role to judge others. We are each the recipient of varying proportions of God's many gifts, and as long as we make use of His gifts, as long as we seek to be good stewards of those gifts, then we are living in a way that is pleasing to God.

For me, this meant going to Church at every opportunity, partaking of the Sacraments, and living an active prayer life. These actions still nourish my soul.

It was certainly an immature relationship at that time, but it was honest and innocent. Through hard work, I had always been able to accomplish my goals. I believed the same held true for getting into Heaven. If I earned enough "points;" prayed enough Rosaries; attended enough Masses, I was sure I would qualify for entry into Paradise. My faith became my road map to redemption, and increasingly, a source of inner peace. This new awakening came just in time.

In June, 1965, I had been with the bank for a year. On one level, I was satisfied. I was working, as my peers were, and making my parents proud. However, on another level, I had questions. "Is this all there is?" I was used to freedom and not constraint. I had enjoyed sports and managing sports teams. I had enjoyed the challenges of entrepreneurship. But now I had little time for anything else but sitting at my desk and doing what other people told me to do. I remember thinking to myself, "Boy, this is a hell of a way to earn a living!"

Whether these subliminal thoughts showed up in my work, I have no way of knowing. I don't think they did. But in June 1965, at my annual evaluation, I was discharged.

My immediate boss in the tax division, the head of the trust department, and the personnel director all sat around a table as I walked in. I felt like I was facing a firing squad. Effectively, that's what it was. They said it was not likely I would move up the corporate ladder. They suggested that I would not be happy staying in the same role for the rest of my career. So, they said, they were doing what was best for me by asking me to leave. They also said my work was seriously affected by what they claimed was my illegible handwriting; which, they claimed, was caused by my disability.

I was out. I would get two weeks of severance pay, during which time I could stay at the bank or leave. I would get the money either way. I left the room, cleared out my desk, and left immediately.

I walked out of the building stunned. It was morning and already hot. I didn't know what to do. I had walked into the same building just moments earlier with a career path mapped out and a feeling that I had achieved, if not happiness, at least respectability. Now, my work life, and the esteem that goes with holding a job, was in pieces.

The first thing I did was go to U.C. to enroll in a typing class. I was in panic mode. The men at the bank, whom I had respected, had essentially fired me because of my handwriting. That was something I could fix. I didn't occur to me that what those men had just done was wrong; that firing someone for behavior related to a disability was not the appropriate or moral course of action. Instead, my insecurity surfaced, and I focused on me, rather than on them. I had a problem. If I worked on it and put enough hours into solving it, I could fix it. That's how I fixed everything else.

Immediately, I dropped by the office of my former accounting professor at U.C. I had no trouble discerning his reaction. He was angry. He recognized instantly the unethical action taken by the bank. Years later, he recalled the words that came pouring out of my mouth that day: "Do you think this is going to happen all the time, again and again? What am I going to do?"

The U.C. typing class wasn't offered at that time, so my next stop was Lockland High School. I approached the typing teacher I had known since childhood. I explained the situation and asked her to enroll me in a summer typing class. She did. I can't help but wonder what she must have been thinking at that time. Was she feeling anger, pity, or affection? For a caring teacher like her, it must have been a difficult situation.

I felt cheated. In that moment my insecurities all came rushing back. This disability, the same one that caused kids to tease me, that had kept me off sports teams, that had led to fruitless job interviews, was always there. It was not going away. There was nothing I could do about it. When I told my parents about what had happened at the bank, I imagine they had the same thoughts.

I had already started my Masters in Business Administration at U.C. the previous September by attending night school several days a week. I decided I would continue working toward the MBA and enroll in a full-time schedule the following September. I had also been asked to coach the girls' softball team from St. James' Parish the previous June. I decided to continue to do that as well.

Then there was the lawn cutting business I had nurtured since I was a boy. Though I didn't actively solicit new accounts, business kept coming my way. In my college years, I would go to school in the morning and then come home and cut grass. I did 379 yards in 1962, and 361 in 1963. It was a source of income that I couldn't take lightly. But now I was twenty-three years old! Was this something I wanted to do for the rest of my life?

I looked around. My childhood friends were putting in fifty and sixty hours of work a week at their chosen professions. They were starting families, buying homes and getting on with their adult lives. I was edging the same sidewalks, trimming the same lawns and knocking on the same doors as I did in the seventh grade. My appetite disappeared and I couldn't sleep at night. I went to the doctor, and he prescribed medicine to calm my stomach. It was a very dark time.

Then I reflected on my faith. Did I have a calling to the religious life? If I decided to move in this direction, how could I be sure it wasn't just a cop-out? How could I be sure I wasn't taking the path of least resistance? I met with several vocation directors and proceeded cautiously, questioning my motives and trying my best to discern what God wanted from me. The vocation directors were also cautious. I was unemployed and unsure of my future. Perhaps they also saw my disability as extra baggage; a hinderance to religious life.

During this discernment period, I began to see God as a loving presence rather than as a force to be feared. If I decided upon a religious life, He would be with me. If I met a special woman and embarked upon a vocation of marriage, He would be with me. If I lived a single life, He would still be with me. My life would not be any easier or more sacrosanct if I were to become a priest. God would not treat me differently. He would love me just the same, and deliver His grace in the same portions.

In all of my consideration of my future, however, I knew I could not go back on the interview circuit. I had had enough of the feigned interest, the fake smiles and the emptiness that followed. I resigned myself to the fact that nobody was going to appreciate my career value in a short interview. They couldn't get past the disability that quickly.

In June of 1966, I finished my MBA. I was probably the only yard man in town to have a post-graduate degree. I believed I had hit rock bottom.

CHAPTER 9
THE ADULT ENTREPRENEUR

When my former accounting professor at the University of Cincinnati learned I had been fired from the bank, he suggested I go into the accounting business for myself. As time went by, and as other options dropped from consideration, I began to think more about his proposal. In addition to his teaching responsibilities at U.C., this professor operated a well-respected tax and accounting business. His confidence in me certainly meant a great deal. I had gained a lot of practical experience preparing tax returns at the bank, and I had a wide circle of Lockland acquaintances, both friends and lawn customers, from whom I could solicit business.

However, it was a daunting prospect. Looking back, the merger of my entrepreneurial history and my finance education made perfect sense, but at the time, it wasn't so clear. A young person starting a business was not nearly so common then, as it is today.

The first step is the hardest. And it *was* hard. But God was with me, shepherding me. In my dark days of 1966, I jumped in head first.

In January, during a time when I had returned to shoveling snow, I began to do a limited number of tax returns. The people for whom I cut grass were my first customers. I worked at a desk in our living room and Mother typed the returns. That first year, I served seventeen clients and cleared $301.

After the tax deadline, I was back to cutting grass. The next tax season wouldn't begin for another eight months. I still had the final few months of my Masters in Business Administration courses to keep me busy; but once I graduated in June, it would be just the grass mowing jobs again. This was a hard period of my life. I took it one day at a time. I put my mind to work, planning for the following April, devising ways to promote my fledgling tax return business.

I had business cards printed, placed ads in the paper, and knocked on doors. Since the local paper carriers did their own billing, I offered to print all their invoices, if they would allow me to put my name at the bottom. They agreed.

Throughout all of this, my parents tried to help me as best as they could. They were careful not to let me sense their apprehension. They were the one constant positive in my life during this time, and I think they knew and appreciated that. My mother, in particular, was worried. In the past she had been concerned that I might not have the capacity to make it on my own in the world. Now she knew I could accomplish just about anything I put my mind to. The question was, "Would anybody give me a chance?"

As the 1967 tax season approached, it appeared they would. Furthermore, realizing a business operated from a living room might not be taken seriously, I looked for an office in the commercial area of our town. My former Boy Scout master operated a coin shop across from the police station, so he let me use the back room of this building. I had a desk, a phone, a couple of chairs, and a typewriter. That was it. But in that year, I began to get a glimpse of my future success. The number of returns increased from 17 to 105. Among those customers were members of my old investment club, former teachers, yard customers and classmates. My gross income was $2,300.

The following year, I completed 324 returns and began taking on the accounting functions for several local businesses. I earned $5,174; that was roughly the amount I had been making at the bank. I had finally turned the corner, and began to get the old entrepreneurial excitement back.

I thank God, not just for the prayers he answered, but also for the ones He didn't answer. Had He led me to a wife and children just out of college, where would I have been when I lost my bank job? How would

I have supported them, or even simply paid the rent? By living at home and remaining single, I had been able to take the business risk and make just enough to get by. Had I needed to support a family during those dark days, I would have taken the first job that came along, even if it meant sweeping floors. God had been protecting me all along.

My practice eventually grew to an average of 2,000 tax returns per year.

CHAPTER 10

THE ADULT SPORTS ENTHUSIAST

From my earliest memories, my father, Frank Grein, and sports are intertwined. Sports were his passion and his relaxation. After six or seven days of straight work, he would set aside time to sit in his recliner, smoke his pipe, and listen to a game on the radio or watch it on television. I would often be right there at his feet.

Yet, for all of Dad's enthusiasm, he never pushed me into sports. He encouraged me to be interested and to participate, but I don't believe he ever associated my worth as his son with any athletic ability I possessed or did not possess. Sports was something he enjoyed, and which he could share with me. It was our common ground and drew us closer.

As I grew older, we went to Cincinnati Reds games together, as well as to the University of Cincinnati basketball games. We talked about sports all the time.

In my youth, sports was the common denominator, both with my dad and with the neighborhood boys. Sports was also a source of division for me. My disability precluded me from participation in organized competition. As a small child I had played sand lot ball and pick-up basketball, but that was as far as my participation could go.

Was I a disappointment to my father? I don't ever recall the question coming to my mind; such was his unconditional love for me. What a blessing that was! I could still be interested in sports, and my worthiness as his son was in no way diminished by my disability.

All through junior and senior high school, I went to all of the school's games: basketball, football and baseball. As the assistant manager, I was an essential member of the teams. I knew the strengths and weaknesses of each player, and I knew the strategies necessary to defeat other teams. I came to know, firsthand, the role teamwork can have in the development of character and self-respect.

Grandma Grein and I had always been close. Conversation between us was easy and I could tell her things I couldn't tell my parents. We often found ourselves together, enjoying one another's company even during my college days. While my classmates were attending fraternity parties or were on dates, I was perfectly content to go with Grandma to softball games. Several of my cousins played ball, and Grandma was their biggest fan.

On one such outing in June 1964, Grandma and I were at St. James, watching a game of the Valley Catholic Girls' League. The St. James' team was, as usual, getting trounced. After the game, the coach was so disgusted with the level of play his team had demonstrated, he quit on the spot! The girls stood around, not sure what to do.

The team's shortstop walked over to the bleachers and, very matter-of-factly, asked me to take over as their coach. The question was so blunt and unexpected that I felt I needed to respond in like manner. I didn't have time to think about the rigid schedule at the bank, where I was still employed, or about the classes in my master's degree program. "Sure," I said. With that brief exchange, I was off on a journey I could never have imagined.

Girls' sports in the early 1960's was significantly different from today's standards. In the Catholic Girls' League, a young woman could only play as long as she remained single. When she married, she had to leave the team. There were no college athletic scholarships available for them. Wearing shorts, even during hot summer afternoons, was forbidden.

As always, I threw myself into the challenge. That first year I performed triple-duty as manager, third base coach and score keeper. We continued to lose, but it was a wonderful year. I totally immersed myself in the sport. The experience helped to carry me through my dark times because coaching was a joy. I felt I was making a difference in young lives. I lived and died with the games.

There were frustrations as well. The fact that the team was made up of young women just shy of marriage age, coupled with the league rule that married women could not play, meant we had a high rate of turnover. Some of the girls had never swung a bat until they walked onto my team. These factors resulted in a great disparity among the players' abilities.

Just as I had done as a kid, I threw myself into the project at hand with great energy and determination. I worked with all the coaches to get the scores posted in the Monday issues of the local newspapers, and sometimes I even did the reporting myself. I worked to expand the league to include new teams, and I helped initiate fundraising projects. I was glad to do all of these things; it was so exciting!

However, I was doing a lot of the work myself. I had to call the coaches for the scores; I was sometimes alone in the fundraising projects; and I wasn't getting paid for all of this work. I didn't have a child on our team; I didn't even have a winning team! Looking back, I now realize that many of the coaches were older and married with children. They also had jobs that kept them busy year-round; whereas I was young, single, and blessed with a tax business that allowed more free time in the summer.

At the team level, I tried to make up for our girls' inexperience by instituting a second day of weekly practice. I was also able to divide the League into two divisions, so even smaller teams would have a chance of winning. I was determined to give our girls the tools and opportunities to make winning possible.

In August 1970, I heard about a tournament in Covington, Kentucky, just across the Ohio River. I decided to create and enter a new team for the competition. I needed many of the all-star players from the other girls' teams.

The difference in play was an eye-opener. With the St. James' team, I was often lucky to have nine players show up for a game. Now, I had the luxury of conducting try-outs with motivated players.

The first game of the tournament was remarkable. I had brought eighteen players that day, in order to have fresh participants, since the games were played one after another. I spent so much time trying to get all of them into those seven innings of that first game that before I knew it, the competition was over. There was grumbling on the bench. These were all-stars; everyone wanted to play – all of the time!

We didn't win the first tournament, but the players and I knew we were on to something. For a team to coalesce so quickly and to play so well, it was only a matter of time before the wins would come our way. I think we all sensed this was just the beginning of something very special.

The tournament also marked the beginning of my relationship with Jake Sweeney, who had built a large and reputable car dealership in our area. After seeing his daughter play first base, and after being impressed with the team as a whole, he agreed to sponsor us for the 1971 season.

Serious coaching can become somewhat akin to monomania. During the heat of the season, I would think, eat, and dream the sport. Victory is the obvious high, but so is camaraderie, the team dynamic, the thud of the catcher's mitt and the smell of a summer ball park.

I was single, had no children, and owned a successful tax business that all but evaporated on April 15. I was left with the spring and summer to move from my vocation of accounting and taxes to my avocation of girls' softball. When the grass was green and the birds were chirping, it was time to play ball!

I was excited to be coaching the new Sweeney team of committed players with a chance for a winning record. However, I knew I would need additional support, so I invited two experienced coaches to join my team. As a bonus, they also helped recruit talented players.

I entered the Sweeney team into a new League sponsored by the Cincinnati Recreation Commission. Other more experienced teams perceived us as pushovers. I knew better.

Our winning team. I'm in the front row second from the right.

My team was made up of some of the best players from our part of town. We went on to achieve thirty wins to ten losses that year. Even more astounding was the caliber of teams we were defeating. Most players were in their 20's and early 30's. In contrast, the Sweeney girls were all under eighteen years of age. Most were only sixteen. And yet, we were winning!

Part of the reason for our winning streak was that our team players had no fear. They were young, cocky, and didn't know to be afraid. They did oddball things because they didn't know any better. They dived for balls and stretched the bases. They were awesome!

On a Sunday in late September, Jake Sweeney invited all of us to his home for a banquet of fine food, remarks and a pool party. It had definitely been a season to celebrate.

In 1972, I formed another all-star team. Everyone was on time for practice, worked hard, and wanted to play to win. We competed in seventy-four games; up from the forty in 1971. Articles were beginning to appear in the newspapers and we soon developed quite a fan-following.

It wasn't unusual to have 500 to 1,000 people in the stands during tournament championships.

The games were like a movie script in which the neighborhood kids knock off the pros. We did so well that in the three major tournaments at the end of the season, we either won the Championship or made it as far as the final Championship game. Our record was sixty wins and fourteen losses, including a stretch where we won twenty-eight out of twenty-nine games!

I have been graced with the ability to largely ignore things that bother me. If there is a confrontation looming, I try to walk away from it. If there are harsh words spoken, I try to ignore them, nor do I dwell on these comments as insults. Perhaps this attitude emerged when I was a child, when I quickly learned there was nothing I could do about taunts regarding my physical condition. So, I had my players promise, both in words and writing, not to say unkind things about whomever was out of favor for the moment. That didn't always work; they were teenage girls, after all!

My mother got tired of the phone ringing and the girls coming over to our house late at night to talk about the current adolescent drama. She made me get another phone, at my expense, and then she said the phone had to go into the basement. In all of my high school and college years, I never had a single female visitor at our house; now my mother was turning them away at the door!

As the 1973 season started, I could foresee a different set of challenges ahead. Instead of parents bringing the girls to practice and the games, the girls were driving themselves. They were also getting jobs and saving money for college the following year. These factors had the effect of causing many to miss practices and games. It wasn't something I could be angry about. It was just a fact of life. The girls were growing older and were moving on.

We won thirty-five games and lost twelve that season. It wasn't only the maturation of the girls that resulted in our lackluster record. Some of it rested squarely on my shoulders.

CHAPTER 11

DISCOVERY OF A DIFFERENT WORLD

In 1971 I joined a tour group in Cincinnati known as "Travel-A-Go-Go." Ever since that trip with my parents to the Rose Bowl and Disneyland in 1958, I had developed a love of travel to new places. In early 1972, at the age of twenty-nine, I went with the travel club to the Mayan ruins in southern Mexico. I had never been to Mexico, and the trip turned out to be one of the most moving experiences of my life; not because of the ruins, but as a consequence of what I experienced on the side trip.

A member of our tour group had been born in Oaxaca, (pronounced waa-haa-kuh) Mexico. He had kept in touch with his family and arranged for our group to go there and participate in a pinata party at The City of Little Children (Ciudad de Los Ninos) Orphanage. We toured the orphanage, which was home to ninety-two boys aged two to twelve. Though the priest, Father Perez, and those who helped him, were doing the best they could with the resources they had available, the conditions in which the boys lived were deplorable.

They slept on boards and rarely took baths, as there was no running water available. Many of the boys had no shoes and wore only the remnants of clothing. Their school classroom was outside.

I was overcome with emotion. I had been dealt the good hand. God had bestowed upon me a wonderful life. I had been an orphan for six months, but was placed with a loving family, and my disability had only been discovered after my new mother came to love me as her own. I had been provided with affection, a warm and safe home, and as much food as I could eat. I had been provided with a good education, a loving extended family, and lifelong friends. When looking at the faces of those small boys, how could my heart not be moved?

This was the first time I had encountered "Third World" poverty. Interestingly, it was also the first time I had met children who, like me, did not know their birth parents. All in all, the effect upon me was profound. I wondered, "Why is God revealing this to me? How does He want me to respond?"

The experience troubled me for the rest of the trip, and continued to do so after I returned home. I was being called to do something, but I wasn't sure what. The question of a religious vocation came rushing back to me. Alternatively, I also considered just dropping everything associated with my present life and returning to Oaxaca to throw myself into the work of the orphanage.

But, too, I had to ponder the gifts God had already given me: my adoptive family, my increasingly successful business, and what I considered to be my ministry through softball. God had always been present for me in all of these blessings. I felt in my heart that He did not in any way fault me for my accomplishments. If I were to pursue a religious vocation, or to exchange my present privileged life for a life of poverty with the orphans, would I not be dishonoring God after He had given me so much? I wrestled with these questions for months.

In the midst of a life-changing experience, I think it is only natural to see options in the extreme, like goal posts in a field. One has to choose; move toward one, and inescapably turn away from the other.

Back home, again immersed in the life I had created for myself, I knew any decision would not be clearly black or white. It would be more complicated than that.

Perhaps God had blessed me, not as an end unto itself, but as a means to help others who have not been so fortunate. "How then," I began to ponder, "could I take advantage of my present circumstances to benefit the orphanage?" I did not have a lot of time to examine these questions. Ball season was fast approaching.

One of my assistant coaches happened to mention to me that

the girls we were coaching were at the time in their lives when their mothering instincts were coming to the fore. Perhaps that is one of the reasons my players always seemed to be concerned about my wellbeing.

So, I presented the idea of collecting needed materials for the orphanage, and proposed the team travel to Oaxaca to distribute them to the kids. I knew the girls weren't just saying "Yes" because of an opportunity to travel. I could tell that my description of the conditions in the orphanage had touched them deeply. I was also aware that they appreciated the depth of my feelings for such an endeavor.

For all of us, it proved to be a lot of work.

We began collecting and buying items that could be of use to the orphanage: clothes, blankets, school supplies, and toys. We sponsored fund-raising games where we played local fire and police teams. We hosted the Lockland Tournament, the proceeds of which were given for the orphanage. I bought the contents of a house as part of an estate auction, and then sold the contents separately. That, alone, raised $20,000. And, of course, we implemented the method of fund raising I had first discovered when I was seven years old: the newspaper drive. In addition, the girls held car washes, painted a house, and started a babysitting business to raise money for the trip.

Our efforts were all the more frenzied because of the date we planned to travel to Oaxaca. My friend had arranged for "Travel-A-Go-Go" to fly us to Mexico at half-price for the girls, and to carry the 10,000 pounds of supplies we had collected. It was an opportunity that couldn't be missed. The date for the flight was August 8, 1973, which left us with only three months to prepare.

The girls had worked hard to pay their portion of the travel expenses and to purchase and collect the needed items. The editor of the Millcreek Valley News reported on the progress of the effort from week to week and encouraged its readers to help. He wrote, "...Now, Roger and these great teen-agers need the help of us in the Valley. They need donations of items such as clothing, shoes, vitamins, toothpaste..."

With such publicity and the dedication of the girls, the momentum of the effort grew. In no time, my parents' garage was filled to the roof with supplies intended for The City of Little Children orphanage. Dad had to park his car on the street!

Although the flight to Mexico City was uneventful, travel after that was anything but! While the regular "Travel-A-Go-Go" members departed for other tourist destinations, our group boarded an old rusty bus for the trip to Oaxaca. The scenery was beautiful, but at times, the route was scary. Our bus rumbled along crumbly roads just inches from sheer cliffs. I recall being somewhat nervous about being in the middle of the jungle with only two coaches and a bevy of high school girls. I didn't know the language of the area and I was unfamiliar with the surroundings. My first trip had been a sight-seeing tour with all the protection and guidance we needed. At that time, we were always able to go back to our hotel for modern conveniences after our excursions. It wasn't that way on this trip.

After enduring eight hours of the bumpy bus ride, we finally reached the City of Little Children and were greeted by Father Perez. From the minute the girls descended the steps of the bus, they fell in love with the little boys. We distributed the supplies we had worked so hard for and then settled in to let the girls and the orphans get to know one another. The mothering instinct of the girls was evident, and heart-warming. It was difficult for them to communicate, at least in words, but that didn't matter. They instantly bonded with the parentless children. At first, the girls tried to strike up a game of softball, with which the boys were totally unfamiliar. Then the boys introduced soccer, with which the girls had no experience. Eventually, a game akin to kick-ball emerged.

I could tell the girls realized that all the efforts of the previous spring and summer had been well worth it; they were making a difference in the lives of these young boys. At that point, I also knew I had made the right decision to continue my life in the Cincinnati area, while at the same time sharing my good fortune with The City of Little Children. I could be more beneficial to them both financially, and by bringing youth from our area to visit.

By the time I returned home, I was drained of all my energy, my commitment to the rest of the softball season was lagging.

I decided to take a trip to the West Coast to attend some away-games of the Cincinnati Reds. I needed time to think about my future and make some significant changes in my softball coaching and managing avocation. I had three options: I could hang up my cleats and move on to other interests; I could continue to coach the Sweeney team; or I could start all over with younger players.

I tossed out the first option quickly. I loved the sport too much to just walk away. The second option I gave considerable thought to, but eventually discarded. The clincher was that the girls were adults now. Coaching adult softball was a whole new "ball game," so to speak. It was more about winning than learning. Thus, it was the third choice, I felt in my heart, to be the right one for me. At the end-of- the-season banquet, I announced to the girls and their parents the difficult decision I had toiled over. I knew I could no longer be their coach.

The 1974 season was one unlike any other. I began recruiting my players one-by-one. They were all aged twelve to fourteen. I wanted to build a true team. By starting a team young, and keeping it together over a number of years, I could see championships in our future. There was an innocent thrill about starting all over. My focus was back. I knew we would likely lose at first, but that was OK. We did lose, but by the end of the season, the girls had coalesced into a strong team, the future of which I knew was going to be bright.

CHAPTER 12

THE MAN THE WHOLE TOWN KNEW

I think most people have a time in their lives when things just seem to click; to come together naturally without conscious design; as if success were a characteristic, rather than an end product. For some people it is falling in love; for athletes it may be several seasons of uncanny play; in short, being in the right place at the right time.

Such a time for me was in the early 1970s. In the summers, the Sweeney Team was beginning its winning ascent. During the winters my tax business was booming. The local Democratic Party asked me to run for the Mayor of Lockland. (I politely declined.) In 1970 I was serving as Tax Commissioner for three small nearby municipalities.

It was at a meeting of tax commissioners during that year that I met the commissioner for Reading. He too operated a small accounting and tax return business. He mentioned that a property in Reading would soon become available for rent. Moving my office from the back of the coin shop to this very prominent location brought my business to a whole new level of success. It was September, 1970 and I was turning twenty-eight years old.

Thanks to this heightened visibility, the next tax season saw a doubling of returns coming through the office. At first, I wasn't prepared. Previously I had relied on my own stamina and my mother's typing to get me through an unexpected number of returns. Now, that wasn't enough. Whereas I had been doing 300-400 returns in a tax season, now 800 were crossing my desk. For the first time, I knew I would need help in the form of conscientious assistants.

I reached out to my assistant softball coach, a gentleman I knew from church, as well as to my cousin. Mother was there to help as well. My lifesaver was a former employee of the bank in which I had previously worked. He was in between jobs at the time and had graduated from Xavier University with honors. He comported himself very well, and just as importantly, was dedicated, punctual and responsible.

When I first asked him if he would like to come on board, he equivocated for some time. Eventually, he said "Yes." He stayed for the rest of his career with me, and also, as an added bonus, helped me with the softball teams. It is to him I owe a large measure of my business success.

During the next few years, my little business continued to grow quickly. With our greater visibility, many of the factory workers from Reading, Lockland and Evendale turned to us for tax advice and return preparation. General Electric, Sterns and Foster, and Philip Carey were dynamic employers for the greater Cincinnati area. When these companies issued their W-2's, we became flooded with customers.

It was a rewarding time for me, but it was not easy. There were many nights I had difficulty sleeping, thinking of the volume of work that had to be completed. I would often get up at 3:00 a.m., and go into the office rather than just lay in bed and worry about what had to be done. Just as my father had worked hard in his roofing business, I was putting in more than twelve hours a day, six days a week.

I must admit, it was a joy! However, being at the top of my game didn't erase the memories of those days when I did not have a job, and when people were hesitant to hire me because of my disability. On the contrary, the doubts and discouragement of those days made my success just that much sweeter. It wasn't something I gloated about, but inside, I felt an abiding satisfaction. My plate was full, and thanks be to God, I had made it on my own - at last.

So business was booming, my softball team was winning and life was good. I had a loving family and a community that valued who I had become. And yet, I still felt like a solitary figure. Perhaps because of my stoic German upbringing, I did not appreciate the need for sharing or speaking frankly about my feelings. But I knew deep down I was missing something. I had grown up, but in terms of my need for companionship, I was still the adolescent wanting a date with a pretty girl.

I was 28 years old and had not kissed a girl, or held a girl's hand since eighth grade. In many ways, my romantic emotions were still stuck in junior high. I felt left out, and I sensed time was running out. I was good old Roger: liked, respected, but still alone. I knew that being single had "saved" me in the mid-sixties by allowing me to be free, take chances and eventually succeed. If I had been supporting a family, I couldn't have risked starting my own company. I also had a full schedule. There were months during tax season when I barely looked up from my desk, let alone have time for a soul-mate. In the softball season, my time was likewise occupied by tournaments, travel arrangements and resolving teenage spats.

Still, when I had time to breathe, I continued to yearn for someone with whom to share my life. I prayed about it, talked to my priest about it, and often thought about it when I was alone. There were single ladies in church I admired, and a waitress at a local restaurant who caught my eye. Once I even joined a dating service, though I never made any calls.

That was the crux of it ---nerve. My batting average was near zero because I hardly ever made it up to bat. I didn't know how to make small talk, ask a girl out, or flirt. It was foreign to me. The same nervousness that had seized me when I was fourteen gripped me still.

I did try occasionally. I would choreograph phone conversations beforehand. I would write down what to say, what topics to discuss, what emergency routes to follow in the event of those dreadful pauses. I usually couldn't eat beforehand, and I always said a prayer first. And while I could keep the conversation going, I seldom had the guts to ask for a date.

At times, I was angry with myself. I could handle defeat on the ball field. I could handle the rejection of a client. However, when it came to asking a woman to spend time with me, my blood ran cold, my hands perspired and the words dried up in my mouth. I felt inadequate.

Through sheer persistence, I did end up taking several women out over a five-year period, but nothing ever clicked. Perhaps I had unrealistic expectations. Interestingly, but perhaps not surprisingly, I always took dates to ball games. I hope they liked sports!

It would be only natural for someone to wonder about my interest in the young ladies on the softball team. The truth is, I never saw them as anything more than ball players, even though we were also friends. I did not allow myself to see them in a romantic light. I took their trust, and the trust of their parents, very seriously.

CHAPTER 13

DAD AND DIAMOND #1

By his nature, my adoptive father, Frank Grein, was introverted. Being of German heritage, he was quiet and stoic. The Great Depression and World War II experiences had made him even more so. I found out years later that he had nearly died during the Battle of the Bulge, and I only learned of this as he reminisced about those days with a buddy. He never shared any of the horrors he experienced during WWII with Mom or me. Like so many of his generation, "The Greatest Generation," he was conservative, prudent, thrifty, patient, trustworthy and obedient to authority - and quiet, very quiet. These were survival traits for bad times, and these qualities would lead him to steadily build a simple, but comfortable life for his family.

When Dad returned home from the war, he returned to work as a roofer, and before long, he had begun his own business. He developed a specialty in tile roofs and was able to attract business in almost all parts of the Cincinnati area. It was grueling work, hour after hour in the hot sun, often working alone, surrounded by hot steaming tar.

Because Dad worked so much, sometimes seven days a week, most of my early memories involve my mother. When home repairs were needed, it was Mom whom I saw wielding a hammer or a screwdriver. When I needed a toy to be fixed, Mom was there for me. She was the predominant force in my life.

Dad was somewhat mysterious to me when I was young. He got

home from work late, often after I was already in bed. Sometimes I didn't see him for days, but I would smell his pipe.

.When I grew older, Dad would occasionally take me with him to watch his buddies play softball. Dad also took me to baseball games to watch the Reds' games at Crosley Field. I also fondly remember those special times when Dad and I would drive off together to do chores. Sometimes I was even allowed to go to work with Dad, where I was entrusted with picking up shingles or carrying tiles.

When I was in the second grade, Dad took me with him to buy a truck for his business. The salesman shook my hand, just like he shook Dad's hand. I felt very proud of my father.

Back then, most fathers showed their love through actions rather than words. My dad worked twelve-hour days so that our family could avoid the grinding poverty he had known in his childhood. Dad didn't speak of love; he kept his emotions to himself, and he was uncomfortable when others openly displayed theirs.

When I was collecting pop bottles and newspapers, cutting lawns and shoveling snow, Dad seldom expressed pride in my work. It would have embarrassed both of us if he had. I am my father's son; I don't express emotion, either. I showed my love for Dad by buying him pipe tobacco at Christmas. Despite the fact that words of affection were not spoken, I knew there was unconditional love between us.

Mom and Dad never moved from their first little house on Moock Avenue. They stayed because of the childhood friendships I had made in the neighborhood. So, from my earliest memories, and even through college, my home life changed very little. I still had the same bedroom and our routines seldom changed; Mom would typically be in the house or out shopping or talking with neighbors, while Dad was usually out on a roof somewhere.

By the time Dad retired in 1973, I had built a thriving business and had winning seasons behind me with the Sweeney Team. Even though I was now a grown man, our relations and expectations of one another remained relatively unchanged. A typical evening would find Dad sitting in his living room chair smoking his pipe, a radio earphone in one ear, with the TV going. Uncharacteristically, Dad developed a keen interest in soap operas!

In 1976, Dad traveled with me when I took the Sweeney Team to Florida. He enjoyed watching the team play, and the day we spent in Disney World. Two years later, he went with the team to Hawaii. Dad and I also had the opportunity to go to more Reds' games together. I was glad to see him enjoying himself.

Then came the fight for Gardner Field!

I had played at Gardner Field as a child, as had all the other children in our neighborhood. It was just a few blocks from our house, and consisted of three softball diamonds and a soccer field. The oldest baseball field, Diamond # 1, sat closest to the road. Outside its first and third base lines, shade trees provided a cool respite from the sun. It was here that Dad would come in the evenings of his early retirement years. He and his friends would sit at the edge of Diamond # 1 and watch whatever ball game was being played. Sometimes he worked as the official scorekeeper, changing by hand the numbers on the old score board. He still never talked about himself, but he was affable; joking almost. He made a point of coming to the Sweeney games and endearing himself to the girls. As was his custom, he kept a little notebook in his pocket to record statistics. Sometimes the girls would go to Dad for their batting averages and he obliged, smiling.

But, it was Gardner Field, Diamond # 1, where Dad enjoyed himself the most. Dad didn't need a gold watch or retirement accolades in return for all his years of work. In a way, fitting of his Depression-era values, he wanted only the pleasure of watching an afternoon ball game from a comfortable seat in the shade.

So, when a turn of events in the spring of 1978 threatened this simple, but important pleasure, Dad reacted in a way none of us could have imagined!

The Lockland City Council received a $190,000 state grant to "upgrade" Lockland's recreational facilities. A consultant from Dayton, Ohio was hired, and within a short time, he recommended the demise of Diamond #1. It was suggested that the ball field be replaced with picnic tables, a running track and a parking lot. The consultant stated that there would still be two ball diamonds left.

Dad was stunned. I felt sorry for him, as I knew the immense pleasure he drew from the ball park. I was sorry to see Diamond # 1 go as well. I had played there, had sat under those shade trees and had organized tournaments there for my softball teams. But it seemed a done deal. I gave the issue a sigh and moved on.

Dad did not. Instead of being quiet, instead of listening and concurring with the established authority, he underwent what seemed a personality change. Before I knew it, he was out in the community rousing the neighbors into action. His name appeared in the local newspaper, then his picture. I didn't know what to think. Mom was shocked as well.

Something had struck a nerve deep within Dad. Maybe it was because it was his beloved Diamond #1. Perhaps it was watching the young "whippersnappers" make "bone-headed" decisions. Perhaps it was a matter of having the time to revolt. I don't know if even Dad knew the reason for his actions. Whatever the motive, he became a changed man. He was a man with a purpose.

Single-handedly, he began a populist uprising, a "Holy War."

He talked to a newsman about how hot it was in the sun at Diamonds #2 and #3. He talked about how he had been hit in the mouth by a foul ball at Diamond #2, causing him to lose several teeth. He talked about the "old-timers," the contributions they had made to the community, and the pleasure they derived from watching ball under the shade at Diamond #1.

When the City Council continued with the plan as recommended by the "expert," Dad went door to door collecting petitions. It became his mission. He wrote letters and he talked with the heads of local political parties. By early summer he had collected 1,000 signatures (close to the voting population of Lockland) in support of retaining Diamond #1. The signatures were presented at a town council meeting, and then ignored. Dad couldn't believe it!

Next, he hired a lawyer. The lawyer handled the paperwork to get the issue on the ballot for the next election. Dad began knocking on doors again. The larger community papers began running articles covering the crusade.

"I'm willing to spend more time collecting signatures," Dad was quoted as saying, "because I feel that the people of Lockland should be allowed to determine if a landmark of the city is destroyed or remains for the pleasure of so many people."

"Good grief," I thought. "Now he sounds like a politician!"

Dad collected the necessary signatures and presented them to the city auditor, who in turn presented them to the Hamilton County Board of Elections.

A local newspaper editor stepped from his usual air of impartiality to issue a signed statement urging Lockland residents to preserve the Diamond. He hinted that the Dayton consultant had more interest in his fees than the well-being of Lockland residents. He implied that dust complaints reported from a small number of residents was nothing but a ruse. Then he wrote, "Frank Grein is a hard-working citizen who earned his retirement. There are literally dozens like Frank who enjoy Diamond #1 and who have earned the right to some enjoyment in retirement. Let's show these fine senior citizens that we appreciate their contributions to our wonderful city by voting to keep their wonderful Diamond. Vote "YES" on Issue 13, and show all concerned that the people still have the power…through the voting booth…to overturn unpopular decisions by those in political power."

The ballot passed by an overwhelming majority with 72% of the voters favoring to keep Diamond #1. Shell-shocked, Council members tried to put their own spin on the vote. The Council president said, "We're supposed to serve the people, so let's serve them. If that's what the people want, it's fine with me."

The edge in his remarks was evident. The Council and its consultant had been defeated by an old man they had treated as a crank; as a modern-day Don Quixote.

The battle over, Dad settled back into his routine. I just had to sit back and smile, incredulously. His fellow old-timers congratulated him, and his new-found adversaries eyed him with respect.

Was this fighting nature, this willingness to challenge authority, something that had always been within Dad? I had certainly never seen it. I questioned, "Has he actually changed from the man he had been when I was a kid?" What did not change was Dad's reticence to talk about himself or express his feelings. When it came to Diamond #1, all he ever said was that it needed saving. And that was that!

CHAPTER 14
A CHANGE IN PERSPECTIVE

My demeanor was like my Dad's. I spoke in terms of facts, figures and dates. I did not participate in idle talk. I listened to authority and trusted institutions. There was no need to share my feelings or emotions. I was a model stoic German grounded in Cincinnati conservatism.

Dad had introduced me to the benefit of retreats in 1956, when I was only fourteen years old. We attended a parish mission offered by Dominican Priests. It emphasized the importance of Mass and praying the Rosary daily. With Dad's encouragement, I found myself growing in my faith.

I began attending daily Mass in 1961, praying my daily Rosary, and offering up other invocations throughout the day. Since my college years, religious retreats had become very important to me, so I set time aside each year to replenish my soul.

I was thirty-seven years old when my outlook on life began to change.

Before 1979, nearly all of the retreats I attended had been offered at the Jesuit Retreat Center just east of Cincinnati. The retreats were silent and for men only. We would listen to a priest's presentation and then reflect upon it in solitude. This pattern would continue throughout the retreat. There was no sharing or voicing our own opinions or feelings on the topics presented. I loved these times away from my busy schedule. This was the kind of spirituality I had grown up with. I knew nothing else.

And then, the windows to my spiritual and emotional life flew open in the Fall of 1979.

One evening I was perusing the newspaper of the Archdiocese of Cincinnati. I noted a small mention about a singles' retreat for men and women ages twenty-five through forty. I had never been on a singles retreat before, much less a retreat with women. The ad intrigued me. It spoke to me in terms of my singleness. I have to admit I considered that perhaps it would be a chance to meet someone special, someone faith-filled.

I called and made my reservation. A week before the retreat was scheduled, I began to have second thoughts. I called the registration office to ask some burning questions: "For the past fifteen years I have been attending silent men's retreats. What is this going to be like? Is this "New Age" stuff?" The lady who answered my call patiently explained that the retreat sought to bring a sense of purpose and belonging to Catholic single people. It had been formulated a year before by the Marriage Encounter movement, with which I was vaguely familiar. She said that everything that was shared was kept confidential, and retreatants could participate to whatever degree they felt comfortable. The three-day singles' retreat was known as "Choice." It began on a Friday evening and the location was a convent near downtown Cincinnati. I was still uneasy. This would not be in my comfort zone. This was not about facts and figures, or listening to clerics in a silent cloistered fraternity.

Upon my arrival on Friday night, I paced about uneasily. I was scared. I wished I was at the Lockland High School football game ---or *anywhere* else. The lady at the registration office had mentioned there would be "sharing." I wondered, "What did *that* mean?"

The retreat was led by three single individuals, one married couple, a Catholic sister and a priest. "Each one of us," we were told, "represents a vocation in life." I listened, but said little. I was surrounded by fifteen other retreatants. I was stuck; I couldn't get out of there!

I listened some more. Gradually, I became interested. As people began to reveal their feelings in small group discussions, I began to identify with some of the things being said. I felt empathy for those talking and was amazed that they were voicing things I had endured, but never verbalized. I was stunned that such things could be talked about --- especially in mixed company!

By Saturday morning I was captivated. I even began to share, not just with my small discussion group, but among the larger group as well. I talked about the priorities in my life, and about the loneliness I sometimes felt. The discussion was wide-ranging and free, but was structured around eleven sessions dealing with everything from life goals to sexuality.

I was astounded by what others shared, and I was surprised by what I was learning about myself. My words revealed the high priority I placed on my faith, and consequently, my belief in Christian service to others. That part came as no new revelation. What I did begin to realize was how limited my close relationships were. For every question that dealt with another human being, I could only list my mother or father as examples. "With whom do you have difficulty communicating?" "My Father." "Who wants to belong to you?" "My mother."

Other retreatants listed a brother, a sister, a friend, a girlfriend or a boyfriend. I had none of those. I had no siblings, but I also had no close friends. I had a whole community of people who knew my name. I was the boy (and then the man) the whole town knew, from my lawn mowing days, paper collecting days, tax business, and my softball teams. But I had no one who knew my thoughts, my sentimental soft spots, my passions, my hot buttons, etc. When I was a kid, I could talk about these kind of things with my Grandma Grein, but when she died, no one had replaced her.

Though this insight might have been a revelation of great sadness, it was instead a joyous discovery. Finally, I had a name for my pain; a diagnosis. The companionship I had sought since I was a teenager, and which I thought would be the end-all to my inner emptiness, wasn't based upon sexuality or the mere presence of another person. It was based instead upon a need to share; just to share. Following in the footsteps of my father, I had never dreamed of telling another person what I felt: what gave me joy and what gave me sadness. Now I realized it was that very reluctance, prohibition even, that had been eating away at my insides. It is human to share. It is human to talk about love and pain. It is essential, and it is very Christian. I knew none of this before October 1979.

In the space of those three days, I learned much more. I learned, for instance, that I wasn't unique. Other people felt just as I did; incredibly so! I could have spoken some of their words. It is a wonder that men and women living under such diverse circumstances, coming from different backgrounds, and levels of faith, can nevertheless reach the same emotional, moral and spiritual conclusions.

The retreat also affirmed for me that there is no easy nor perfect vocation. There is no fast-track to the gates of St. Peter. Whether a person is ordained, is a member of a religious order, or is married or single; we all have vocations. These life choices all have joys, trials and tribulations. Regardless of the vocation one is living, he or she is still the same person, and we are all still stuck or blessed with the same weakness and strengths. This realization alone lifted a weight from my shoulders. Ever since graduation, I had felt a twinge of insecurity, as my buddies married and started families of their own. I sensed I was missing out, not growing, and falling behind. Since the retreat, I no longer saw it that way. No matter what my life course might have been, I would still have ended up the same person in God's eyes.

When I walked out of the convent Sunday afternoon, I felt a sense of excitement and relief. I finally had the old insecurities washed away. It was such a freeing experience. Interestingly, I had never had a moment or reason to mention my softball avocation to my fellow retreatants.

I arrived home still on cloud nine. I think my parents may have believed I was on drugs. A letter I had written to them during the retreat arrived a short time later. In it I told them how much I loved them and how much I appreciated their presence in my life. My dad just looked at me without saying a word. Mom was worried. "What did they do to you?" she asked.

The letter was my first attempt to open the door to them; to have an honest dialogue with them. It was the beginning of what would be a lifelong process.

I can't imagine my life without having had the experience of this retreat in 1979. Perhaps some other circumstance might have come along to uncork my pent-up feelings and insecurities, but God's timing was perfect. I trust that this was His plan all along.

Many of the retreat leaders, and the fifteen other retreatants, and I have remained close friends. They have proven to be one of my support groups. I can talk to them from my heart; I can be open and vulnerable with each of them, without experiencing embarrassment or shame.

Shortly after we parted that weekend, I called or wrote to just about all of them. I had wanted to say, "Thank you." I also attended a follow-up evening two weeks later.

On New Years' Eve, 1979-1980, I went on a double date with one of the retreat leaders. I'll call her Peggy to protect her privacy. The four of us went to dinner and then back to Peggy's home to play cards. We all conversed freely. It was a new world for me!

CHAPTER 15

THE SPECIAL ONE

Peggy. For me, it was the most powerful word in my vocabulary. I felt like Tony singing "Maria" in West Side Story. I couldn't hear it on the television, see it in print, or use it in reference to another individual without thinking of *my* Peggy.

As a child and young man, I had been infatuated with Carol, and mostly from a distance. But with Peggy, I was really in love for the first time. I was thirty-seven years old.

It's funny how love can sneak up on you. I met Peggy at the singles' retreat, but I felt no special attraction for her at that time. I was so overwhelmed by the subject matter and the new perspectives it was drawing out of me, that for the first time in years, the subtle but persistent search for a companion had not been in focus.

Even afterward, when I was calling retreat leaders to thank them for the experience, I hadn't recognized Peggy as anyone special, probably because there had been several other compassionate individuals who had walked me through the weekend. I knew I was comfortable around her and that she was easy to talk to. Even when I asked her out for New Year's Eve, I'm not sure I had any thoughts of a relationship. I was just spreading my wings, and reveling in my new-found ability to discuss topics other than business.

In 1979, Peggy was a dental hygienist living in Cincinnati. In her spare time, she taught religion classes to the youth of her parish. She had moved from a town north of the city, where her father still lived.

She was a twenty-six-year-old slim brunette, and possessed a demeanor that was spontaneous and sociable.

I called Peggy several times shortly after New Year's Eve. She was the first woman I could call on the phone without getting nervous. In mid-January, 1980, I asked her out again for a dinner date. This time it was just the two of us, and I began to think of her as more than a casual friend.

Perhaps Peggy sensed my growing fondness for her, and perhaps she was starting to think of me differently as well. During dinner she made a point of telling me she had recently ended a serious relationship, and suggested that she was not ready to start another one just yet. I was enjoying the moment and not taking anything for granted. If we were just going to be friends, I was OK with that for the time being. That was more than I had ever had before.

In February, we continued seeing one another. I called her two or three times a week and our conversations were easy. We went to Ash Wednesday Mass together, and then afterward, to dinner. There was no romance, but I could tell she enjoyed my company. I certainly enjoyed hers.

At the end of February, I asked Peggy to go to the circus with me. I remember nothing about the show, but I remember holding her hand as we sat there. It was warm and soft and given freely. I savored the moment. I will never forget that night.

I know some would smile at my middle-aged innocence. After all, the thrill of holding hands is something most people associate with junior high. I had held hands with a girl once before in eighth grade, but not since then.

Now, at age thirty-seven, I felt like an adolescent. On the intellectual level I saw Peggy as someone I was attracted to, someone whose company I enjoyed, and someone who shared my faith. On another level, I was a smitten high school kid.

After the circus, I took Peggy home. I hadn't worked up the nerve to kiss her, so I just gave her a big hug. I would like to have stayed with her longer, but I knew the amount of work that was building up on my desk. It was mid-tax season after all, and my company was in high gear.

If there was ever a time NOT to fall in love, it was mid-February. I already had 800 tax returns to get out the door, and that number was likely to double by April 15. My only days off during tax season were Sundays. I usually spent Sunday afternoons processing payroll, paying bills and sending out invoices.

I was also in the middle of planning another trip to Mexico with the Sweeney Team, as well as bringing the softball World Championship to Cincinnati for the fast-approaching summer. To top it all off, practice was due to begin. Alas, love does not seem to care about schedules.

It was hard to sleep that night after our date to the circus. I was too excited about my future with Peggy. I thanked God and asked for His guidance. I wondered if, after my long wait, Peggy was the one I would spend the rest of my life with.

A few weeks later, Peggy asked me to meet her father. Her mother had died when she was young. He was retired and a deacon with his church. She showed me the house where she grew up, then took me for a short walk through the woods she frequented as a child. There was a path that ran along a creek.

Peggy stopped at a big rounded rock at the edge of the water. She climbed up and beckoned me to follow her. It was a beautiful spring day; the flowers were blooming and the sun was glorious. I sensed this was a special place for Peggy, and I was glad she had decided to share it with me.

The sun was shining upon Peggy's long brown hair, and she was smiling. Her eyes were warm and inviting, and when I gazed into them, I felt like I had never felt before. I was struck by her beauty. I could have held her and kissed her, but I didn't. I was happy just watching her and listening to her voice.

From that moment until the end of March, I spent every free moment with Peggy. Sunday afternoons would often find me at her place. I invited her to meet my parents. I was in an emotional state I had never experienced before.

And then, as new couples sometimes do, we paused. Peggy needed time to think about our relationship. In the span of two and a half months we had gone from a casual acquaintance to an emotional attachment that surprised us both.

We agreed to stay apart through Holy Week. That included no phone calls. We agreed to think about what had happened and in the quiet spaces, decide how we each wanted to move forward.

The brief separation was necessary for Peggy, but I didn't need it. I could certainly use the time to focus on my business. The tax deadline was fast approaching. Then, on April 30, my first quarter payroll, sales tax and bookkeeping reports were all due. It took all of my fortitude to stay on track and remain disciplined.

But even as busy as I was at work, the first day of our separation ticked by slowly. In a moment's lapse of concentration, my mind would slip back to her and I would recall her sweet voice. She had become everything that was beautiful to me. I wanted to share my life with her. I was a new person with Peggy, and I knew she loved me. She even tolerated my frequent talk about sports. That was no small forbearance.

I had promised not to see or call her, but I knew I couldn't last the week. I wondered if she were having the same problem. "Give her some time," I told myself. "Be patient. Love is being patient, right? Buckle down, catch up on work, and grow up!"

Although we had not discussed writing, I knew a full letter would break the spirit of our agreement. But, I wanted to give her a sign. I wanted her to know that being without her was not easy, that even when I was focused on work, she was on my mind. I wanted her to know I was feeling this way every minute of every day we were apart.

I pulled out some small stationary and I wrote the word "I" and sealed the envelope. With no return address, I put a stamp on it and mailed it to Peggy. The next day, on another piece of stationary, I wrote the word "love." Again, I mailed it with no return address. Over four days, she got the complete message; "I love you, (from)Roger." But even before I could get the whole message relayed, I began receiving messages from her. They were in the same vein. I knew then I was on the right track. I knew that our hiatus had been hard for Peggy too, and that she loved me!

I decided to propose.

Peggy invited me to her father's house for Easter, where each year her extended family gathered. During my last visit there, we had walked in the woods and sat by the stream. I had thought at that time, "What a great place for a proposal!" In all the world, it was her most treasured spot.

All through the meal and conversation, I was anxious about how I could arrange our departure to walk into the woods. I was concerned about having the atmosphere just right, and I never contemplated rejection.

We finally made our escape into the woods. Again, the sun was shining. The forest floor was green with spring growth, and the trees had the hints of their first leaves. When we reached the rock by the spring, I asked Peggy to marry me.

She looked at me intently. The time between when I asked the question and when I first saw her lips begin to form an answer seemed an eternity. I felt anticipation, elation and panic all mixed together. "Give me time to think about it," was all she said.

My part was over and I felt relieved. She had answered me kindly, sensing my nervousness and trying to soothe it. Now the ball was in her court. I had to respect that. She needed time to think, pray and reflect upon how she wanted to spend the rest of her life.

That night we ate dinner with my parents and aunt and uncle. On the drive over, she mentioned how her brother had met someone special and had become engaged quickly. I took her comment as a positive sign.

After dinner we went for a walk. Our conversation was easy. My proposal had not divided us in any way. I took that for another positive sign. Peggy was so special to me. I had to respect whatever she decided, but I didn't want to lose her.

Both of us kept the proposal private among our family members. Rejection would be a bitter pill, and even more so if those who loved me knew about it.

After several days, though, I did feel a need to talk to someone about my angst. I had noticed an Engaged Encounter retreat scheduled in our community, and I wondered if such an event could help Peggy reach a decision. I spoke to the associate pastor at my parish who happened to be the priest assigned to the retreat. I asked him if attending was acceptable for couples just considering marriage. He said it certainly was and had been done many times before.

Looking back, I acknowledge some duplicity on my part. On one hand, I knew Peggy had to reach her own decision. On the other hand, I thought the experience might cajole her to reach a decision in my favor. I would be in her presence during the retreat, and if she expressed any doubts, I would have time to respond immediately. I desperately wanted her decision to be a resounding, "Yes."

Peggy agreed that the retreat would be a good idea. She was aware that we would be forced to take time out of our busy schedules and address the question of marriage head on.

The retreat was scheduled to begin Friday evening and go through Sunday afternoon. Peggy met me at my parents' house. I had a dozen red roses waiting for her, so she held the flowers and posed with my father for a photo.

There is something about adding a special person to your family that is indescribable. It is a feeling of joy and pride. Peggy was a gift to me and my parents. I was as happy as I could ever recall.

During the retreat I was glad to be with Peggy and to be talking about our future. There was structure, with questions prompting a written response to be shared privately. I tried to be honest, but was still nervous. If Peggy would just say "Yes" everything would be wonderful.

At one point during the retreat, Peggy confided to me that she didn't know if she could have children. I could tell the words had been hard for her to say.

I certainly understood her concern, but being an adopted child, having grown up with unconditional love, I knew there were good alternatives to this potential issue. I told her, even if we decided not to adopt, I would still love her and want to grow old with her.

The following evening, after the Engaged Encounter retreat, I was scheduled to begin my annual Jesuit retreat. It would last until Wednesday. I thought of how much work was on my desk. I was getting behind, and wondered if I had enough energy to handle everything.

Peggy occupied all of my thoughts, yet my work deadlines were still impending. Another Mexico trip was fast approaching, softball try-outs had already begun, and many details concerning the World Championship Tournament needed to be resolved. My schedule stood before me like a set of iron bars, unmoving. I wondered how I could do it all, especially if I kept taking time off for retreats!

Even in the midst of my anxiety and my restlessness to get moving, I knew my time management skills and discipline could only get me so far. I would need God's grace and an energy only He could give me to make it through. I decided to make the Jesuit retreat. Too, it would give Peggy some space to reflect on what I thought had been a very positive experience for both of us. I never dreamed, though, how she would make use of her time.

The Jesuit retreat ended Wednesday afternoon. Peggy had an appointment with her spiritual advisor at 8:00 p.m. that same night. We decided to meet and get a bite to eat before her appointment. After dinner we took a short walk in the woods near her apartment. Suddenly she turned to me and said, "Yes, Roger, I will marry you."

The air was warm and it was still light. I kissed her. It was wonderful.

I went with Peggy to her meeting with the priest, but rather than discussing spiritual direction, we talked about a fall wedding. It was like a dream.

I went home and told my parents. I felt like a kid again. I shared their pride and their happiness. That night, as I lay awake, I thought of Peggy and the road ahead.

So, now I was engaged!

Each day after work, Peggy and I would meet. We were becoming used to one another. We could have comfortable silences, as well as conversation. We simply enjoyed one another's company. We would wash dishes after a meal and just sit together watching television. I could not have imagined such a relationship just a year before. We were becoming a family. On Opening Day (a big deal in Cincinnati!), we took our fathers to the Reds' game.

I was also, for the first time in my life, allowing my sexual self to awaken. I knew that Peggy and I would be able to physically consummate our love in the Sacrament of Marriage. I began to think about that. I had over two decades of pent-up desires to love and be loved, both emotionally and physically. I shared my anticipation with Peggy and was honest about my lack of experience.

With everything in my life, from riding a bicycle to being able to make a living, I had always found myself behind everyone else. I knew I was slower than my peers in many areas; regarding romance, it was no different.

I still had doubts about my future. I was concerned about how I was going to juggle my commitments. The players on the ball team had become my family. Already, I felt I was limiting my time with them because of my focus on Peggy. Before, I had always given the team 110% percent of my energy and time. Could I do that with a wife?

I had spent fifteen years as a coach, and we had won the World Championship in 1978. To give it up now would be a huge sacrifice.

Peggy had supported the team and my involvement with them. She had come to most of our games and kept the hitting chart for the opposing team. But if she changed her commitment to our team, what would I do?

I also had the age-old feeling of cold feet. I had never dated seriously before and wondered if by marrying, I would be forgoing other potential women in my life.

I talked to a priest about all of my concerns and my feelings of guilt. The priest advised me that it was normal apprehension, and not to worry.

It was about this time when a woman I'll call Betty, walked through my door. She was a widow and her daughter was joining our team. Betty was the most beautiful woman I had ever seen. She was petite and slender with short dark hair. Her skin was tanned and she wore a simple spring dress. She looked like a model. I was stunned before she even opened her mouth. My heart was thumping; my composure was in question. When she began to speak, her voice was calming and cool.

"God, what are you doing to me?," I thought.

I could not deny my attraction to Betty. I couldn't deny that I would look forward to seeing her again in the stands. I might even go out of my way to talk to her after the games. Was this normal for an engaged man?

I also had concerns about my living arrangements. I was still living with my parents. My mother was cooking my meals as well as making my bed each morning. My dad was always there to share the latest baseball scores with me. How would it be with my own mortgage, my own grocery shopping and other domestic responsibilities?

And while these pesky thoughts buzzed about my head, Peggy and I continued our journey. We picked out a ring and drove through the neighborhoods looking at houses. At times I feared that my doubts might manifest themselves in some way. Did they make me distracted or anything less than loving?

At the end of May, Peggy's cousin was getting married in Chicago and I decided to fly with Peggy and her father to attend. Peggy was in the wedding party, and as I watched her walking up the aisle, as beautiful as I had ever seen her, I had to smile. The next wedding would be our own!

I think Peggy must have had some of the same feelings. When we arrived back in Cincinnati and returned to her apartment, she was affectionate with me as never before. She caressed me, stroked my hair, and leaned into me on the couch. I wanted to be with her and to forget about everything else, but the treadmill in my brain was still running. I was dealing with softball tournament contracts, my tax business and my approaching trip to Mexico.

She asked me to stay, as I prepared to leave for practice. I was already late and the Sweeney Girls were waiting.

During the next few days, I felt like a man unhinged. There was too much to do and think about. I felt I couldn't breathe.

Then, a major tornado hit Cincinnati! It threw cars around and twisted light poles. As it passed my office building, it sucked out the windows and in its fury, spit great globs of debris and dirt into my offices. It tossed the furniture and machines around like small toys. By the grace of God, the tax records were spared. But I was not. I was a wreck. The Mexico trip was only a week away.

To this day, the first week of June 1980 remains a blur to me. I shoveled dirt off my desk, swept giant shards of glass from the office, and pitched what used to be office machines into the jumbled shoulder-high piles of debris lining the curbs of our street. I filed my property insurance claims, tried to manage details of the upcoming Sweeney-hosted World Championship, and nailed down the Mexico trip. I hardly had a chance to see or speak to Peggy or anyone else.

On June 8, twenty-nine softball players, their parents and friends, Peggy and three other members of the Singles Group and I, took off for Mexico. We were scheduled to be there a week. Our itinerary called for a four-day visit in Mexico City, where the Sweeney Team would compete with four of the best girls' softball teams in the Mexican Sports Federation. Then we would fly to Oaxaca and the City of Little Children - the orphanage that had stolen my heart seven years before.

I was excited about the trip. Peggy was beside me, holding my hand as we traveled. I was fulfilling what had become a personal mission of supporting the orphanage. It was time to count my blessings. What had kept my mind on Mexico, and what brought me back now, were the small faces of the orphans, that, even amidst extreme poverty, were always smiling.

There was a bond that had developed among us. For whatever reason, each of these children had been left without parents. In my early months of life, I too had been set aside, but unlike these children, I had grown up in a land of plenty. I knew a loving home with Frank and Thelma. I always had plenty to eat, clothes to keep me warm, and hope for a happy future. God had blessed me even when I was in my mother's womb.

So, when I was with these children, my mind often turned to the thought, "There, but for the grace of God, go I." Truly, God had smiled upon me, and now I felt He was calling me to pass along His beneficence. It was an obligation of joy and one I was now excited to share with my life's companion-to-be, Peggy.

Our plane touched down in Mexico City around mid-afternoon. My friend, Raphael, had taken it upon himself to arrange much of our

Mexico City itinerary. He had arranged the softball schedule and a number of sightseeing trips.

The next two days we explored the city in the mornings and played ball in the afternoons. Peggy smiled at everyone and endeared herself to the street vendors with her few words of Spanish. She smiled at me with a twinkle that said she was mine. It is a picture in my mind I will never forget.

Yet, for all of my desire to be close to Peggy, and to enjoy our new relationship in this romantic place, it was a challenge to find time to be alone with her. I was a coach and tour guide for our entourage, so I had to make sure meals and transportation were arranged every day.

We managed to win every game in Mexico City! I was so proud of how well the team played as representatives of our nation.

Then it was on to Oaxaca! On my first visit, in 1973, we had taken an eight-hour bus ride to get there. I decided not to repeat that torturous mode of transportation. This trip, we flew there from Mexico City, and arrived a short time later.

In 1980, Oaxaca was a raw provincial capital of what amounted to a third-world region. On the dusty, garbage-strewn streets, vendors hung great slabs of meat, and young children were begging at our elbows constantly. I had been exposed to this before, but the others had not.

That night we ate at an outdoor café. The food was good, the music Latin, and the drink free-flowing. Some of the parents made puerile sexual comments about Peggy and me. We could only blush and smile.

The next day we set out in a bus for the City of Little Children. I was excited. I had made financial contributions regularly since my last visit, and had stayed in touch with them through communication with my friend, Raphael. I had always kept the children in my prayers. I looked forward to holding them in my lap and playing with them once again.

In 1973, there had been no electricity, no plumbing and no phone. From the looks of things, that was still the case. These kids lived in a type of poverty unimaginable in the United States.

The priest continued to spend every minute of his spare time providing for his orphans and the home he had created for them. He was doing much of the physical labor himself that was necessary to put food on the table and provide the bare necessities. His local support came from his Oaxaca parish and friends.

The children enjoyed love, a place of security and they were not homeless. School and religious education were available to them. True, they slept on boards and ate outside, but what was the alternative? There was no support for them from the Mexican government. The City of Little Children was on its own. If Father was unable to raise enough money in any given week, the children went hungry.

Raphael told me about one boy's experience. He had been found unconscious in the bushes by the highway. His jaw was swollen and filled with infection. He was about eight years old. He was brought to the orphanage, where a doctor drained the infection. The boy survived and was welcomed by the City of Little Children. Other boys had experienced similar horrors.

When I came the first time, I considered giving up my life in America and living with the children, but I quickly realized that it would be little help for the orphans. On the other hand, if I used the gifts God had given me - my financial success and my ability to persuade others to donate, then I could make more meaningful contributions.

Watching the high school girls playing with the young boys, I knew they could learn a lot from this experience. The girls could learn how blessed they were; both in terms of family and material gifts. I wanted them to appreciate their own gifts and consider how they could use them to brighten the lives of others.

So, this time, I prepared my girls to meet the children who had touched my life so much seven years earlier. As we pulled up, nearly a hundred small boys rushed out to meet us. I was so glad to be back.

As it had happened with the previous visit, the girls immediately connected with the little boys. They couldn't speak the same language, but they interacted just the same. The girls attempted soccer and the boys attempted softball. Later we attended Mass, with the boys carrying flowers up the aisle. Once again, we had a pinata party with the orphans and the Sweeney Girls blind-folded and flailing sticks at the cache of candy hung from one of the few trees. Everyone had a good time.

Occasionally I would look at Peggy, who was sometimes close to me in the crowd. Often she had a child in her arms with a warm smile on her face. She was simply glowing; I knew I would love her always.

The next day, Raphael had scheduled a softball game with the boys from a private school in Oaxaca. One thing that is very obvious in this part of Mexico, is the great disparity of wealth. Most of the population is poor, but there are a few fabulously rich residents. Many of the Sweeney Girls were staying in the homes of these wealthy families. I wondered about the justice of a society that allows children to starve when plainly, there are resources available to provide them with a minimum sustenance.

The local newspaper reporter arrived and took a team photo, then individual shots of the girls. These photos were published prominently in the Oaxaca paper.

Despite playing fast-pitch against a team of boys, the Sweeney Girls still won rather easily. I guessed that the boys had heard we had recently won the World Championship, so their feelings didn't get too bruised.

Shortly after this game, I began feeling weak. My muscles began to ache, my stomach cramped, and I went to lie down. As time passed, I felt worse. A fever came on and then uncontrollable vomiting followed by diarrhea. I lived the rest of the day and night in bed or in the bathroom. Peggy came to comfort me the best she could.

I drifted in and out of consciousness. In my few lucid moments, I felt embarrassment. Peggy and I were a newly engaged couple and still learning about one another in so many ways.

This one way, however, we both could have done without.

When it was time to board the plane for Mexico City, I was leery about leaving my room and the toilet that had become my constant companion for the previous thirty-six hours. I looked like a ghost, but at least, I hoped, I could travel.

On the way home I reflected on our trip. I felt disappointed that Peggy and I had spent so little time together. There are photos of us holding hands and standing close. But most of our time had been filled with other people with no private time for one another. There had been no time or opportunity for romance.

I was glad to have the trip behind me and the sickness almost over. There was the ball season ahead, and Peggy to cherish. We knew each other better now, and I loved her even more. We might face bumps ahead and new feelings to sort out, but I felt sure we could work them out.

"I don't think this is going to work," she said. She slipped the ring from her finger and handed it to me saying, "I don't think we were made for one another." She looked at me a moment then lowered her eyes slightly, so that she was just looking forward. I searched her face for more, but there was no more. I just stood there. Thirty seconds before, I had been noticing the woods, walking easily along the trail where Peggy and I had often visited. Then she turned to me, and the whole world turned upside down.

It was ten days after our return from Mexico. I had no clue in all that time that anything was amiss. We had arrived back in Cincinnati on a Sunday and Peggy had not come to the Tuesday ball game. I was still tired, and thought she might be also. On Wednesday, we went to a restaurant and had an enjoyable time together. Over the weekend, we went swimming. In my mind, we were returning to normal engagement activities. Obviously, I was missing something. It was the following Wednesday when she gave the ring back to me.

I don't recall how the silent shock was broken. Perhaps something more was said, but my mind has blocked it out. We turned around and walked the fifteen minutes back to the car. I felt a sense of doom.

That night we had agreed to eat supper with my parents. I set my jaw and went through with it. Nothing was said during dinner about the engagement being over. I felt like I had just learned of a terminal illness and had not yet shared the news. I heard myself talk as if from a distance. Later that evening, on the front porch, Peggy told my parents. I did not look at her face or the faces of mother and father. I couldn't.

In bed that night I felt like I was suffocating. There was no way I could escape from what had just happened. There was no thought that could distract me; no silver lining.

My mind mulled over every detail of the evening; every word that had been spoken. What had happened? It had been a few short weeks since we returned from the wedding in Chicago, when Peggy had shown such love and affection for me. Now she didn't want me at all!

"It was Mexico," I thought. It had to be. Nothing else had happened in the time between when everything had been perfect and the rejection on the path in the woods. I had wanted to share my great affection for the orphans with her. Instead, it had cost me her love. I know I had been a mess that trip. I had been pulled in so many directions, with no time for romancing Peggy. I had spent my energy on the ball team, the issues of the girls and their families, the World Championship Tournament, the orphans; and then I got sick. I had tried to cram everything in at one time. I should have allowed someone else to take the lead on that trip. That would have given Peggy and me more time to enjoy one another.

I began to talk to God. "Why are you doing this to me? I wanted to do so much for the orphans and so much for the Sweeney Girls. Haven't you dealt me enough misfortune?"

The next day I tried to go through my regular routines. I went to work and prepared for a game that night. I felt like a dead man walking. If I could figure out what went wrong, then I could fix it. I was the fix-it man! Given time and my mechanical nature, I could make anything work. That's how I learned to ride a bike and climb a tree. That's how I excelled as a coach when I couldn't make it as a player. That's how I had become successful with my own business when my first employer fired me.

I began to wonder, "Is it my disability that's the problem?" Because of my spastic condition, I am not as dainty as others. Despite years of working at it, and despite much concentration when I butter my bread or cut a piece of meat, I still am not the ideal model for table etiquette. With effort, I can pour a glass of water, but I don't attempt coffee. I can hold a drink and walk across a room, but only if the glass isn't too full and only if I concentrate. I slurp my soup and slop my milk. It's just the way my hands and mouth function because of my cerebral palsy.

Could it be that such actions, and other quirks of my disability, had finally gotten to Peggy? We had never discussed my spastic behavior, as it never seemed pertinent to our relationship. Perhaps the "elephant in the room," was something we should have addressed. When we were in Chicago at the wedding reception, I sat out some of the fast dances. My lack of coordination wouldn't have allowed my participation. Early in our relationship, I bought a book about how to kiss, but had caught on pretty quickly. Peggy seemed to enjoy my kisses, so I didn't think that was the issue.

There have been times in my life when my disability angered me, but I had grown out of that. By the grace of God, I have always had an innate realization of the many blessings in my life; blessings that far out-weigh any physical shortcomings I may have. I adapt when I can, and when I can't, I don't waste any time thinking about it or feeling sorry for myself.

Now, on this morning after Peggy's rejection, a bit of anger began to creep into my mind. Would this thing, this condition of mine, haunt me for the rest of my life? I began to shiver with that thought. However, after a few moments of my morning prayer, God gave me the mental fortitude not to have a pity party. He allowed me to think clearly, and in doing so, dismiss the issue. Just two weeks before, Peggy had loved me, physical limitations and all. I knew that even if these had been things she thought about, she had overlooked them and loved me.

I decided I could not look at my disability as a scapegoat. The cause of Peggy's change of heart couldn't be that easy to find. If I didn't know what the core problem was, I couldn't repair the damage and make things right. I was determined to find out.

During the next pre-game huddle with my Sweeney Girls, after we said our team prayer, I told them what had happened. Then we all slapped hands and the game was on.

When Peggy had told me the engagement was off, she also intimated that the relationship was also off. There were tears in her eyes when she told me. I didn't get the impression that she no longer cared for me, but that there could be no retreat into friendship. It was better to make a clean break. My mother, with both kindness and hurt in her eyes, told me the same thing. "Let go of her," she said. "If you are not going to marry, both of you have to move on."

It still bothered me. What had gone wrong? Peggy had given me no details, and I couldn't fix what I didn't know was broken. I knew better than to call Peggy, but I had to slap my hand away from the phone many times. I did call some of our mutual friends, both to inform them of what had happened, and to ask them if they knew of any clues I was missing. If I could only discover what I had done wrong, I would move the Earth to fix it.

For several weeks after, I remained in a fog. Peggy had charmed everything, and I often found reminders of her. There were the restaurants we had gone to, and the park paths we had walked. I often thought, "This is the time I would have been with her." I was devoid of hope and positive expectations. I am told there are five stages in the grieving process: disbelief, bitterness and anger, bargaining, and finally, acceptance and growth. I was in the first three stages. I was crucifying myself for a calamity I believed could have been avoided, and I was bargaining with God for some kind of reprieve. "God, where are you?" I prayed. I felt like I was on a rope, sliding downward, and God was the last knot I could hold onto before losing myself into the abyss.

My faith came through for me. I was able to hold on to God, so I did not crawl into a shell and hide. God was with me. The Sweeney Girls were with me. All was not darkness.

Much was expected of us as the Sweeney team began the 1980 season. Eight teams were entered in our age division of the tournament. We won each of our four games, including the final game 15-1. Since there was little happening on the field, I occasionally scanned the stands for Peggy. She was never there.

I had a pre-scheduled appointment with my dentist to put on a permanent crown. As Peggy was still working in that office, I thought I might see her. She was not needed for the procedure, but as I was leaving, I saw her at her desk. I said, "Hello," and walked out the door.

The Sweeney team continued to win games, but Peggy was not there to share my joy. I missed her physical companionship, her warmth, and most of all, I missed sharing my thoughts and feelings with her. She had been my first confidant. For thirty-seven years I had lived without such a person in my life, and then, after three short months, I had lost her.

Finally, the softball season was over. It had been hard to keep my head up, and to think of anything other than Peggy. I also knew that the team had been my salvation. They had given me something to latch onto. The girls and the challenges of the games had been my life preserver.

I finally decided to make contact with Peggy. It was simple enough. Just a postcard. It was the first time in seven weeks I allowed myself to reach out to her. I did not hear back from her.

I called the Jesuit retreat master to see if I could make two retreats that year; one in September and one in January 1981. I needed strength, and I knew no better way to get it than to renew my relationship with Christ. It could only be God who would get me through this desert period in my life.

During the first retreat, there were talks by priests, followed by quiet time to reflect and pray. I also made time to talk to the retreat director and fill him in on Peggy and Mexico. I felt great relief to share my pain with him. I prayed to God and said I was open to whatever He wanted of me.

In October, 1980 I made another retreat with the singles group. This time I was a team leader. I had certainly grown during the last year in terms of sharing with others. I knew what it was to love someone special, and to lose that love. Perhaps I had learned enough to help others. In my talks, I made no mention of Peggy. Curiously, I met a girl there who had recently gone through much the same pain as I had experienced. We talked at length, knowing how important it was to listen and how healthy it was to share. I took her out twice later. Perhaps I was beginning to move on.

By November, I was beginning to accept, to heal and to grow. It had been five months since our broken engagement. I had respected her wishes for separation. In December, I called Peggy and invited her to a performance at Music Hall. To my surprise, she enthusiastically agreed. I was careful not to read too much into her acceptance. I had grown a lot since last June, but I still hoped she would again be mine...eventually.

Betty, whose appearance in my office the previous May had shaken me, was also present at the concert. We exchanged a few words with her before leaving the venue. On the way to my car Peggy said, "Roger, that is someone you should definitely be interested in." First, it was the irony that hit me; then the pain, knowing the relationship with Peggy was really over.

CHAPTER 16

MOVING ON

All my life, one of my greatest desires, one of my greatest needs, has been to be accepted and loved. I learned over time that the best way to gain that love is to be loving toward others. I cannot say that I have not received my fair share of love. My biological mother had the resolve to bring me into this world. My adoptive mother, even after discovering her perfect baby was in some way "broken," loved and supported me always.

The other faces of love, however, have not easily come my way. The face of a lover, the face of a son or daughter; these have escaped me. I still had a hunger for such loves.

In their place, I had my softball teams, my faith, and my church community. I would never have been able to help the orphans in Oaxaca if I had had children of my own to shelter, feed and love.

The point was driven home to me in June 1982. The Sweeney girls presented me with a card expressing their appreciation and affection. The written expressions from all fifteen of the girls were nice, but it was the outside of the card that got to me. It was a Father's Day Card.

The Sweeney girls were in many ways like my children. I had watched them grow up. I not only studied their strengths and weaknesses on the field, but I knew about their lives off the field, too. I knew how they were doing in school and what their aspirations were for life after graduation from high school. I shared their joys and sorrows, just as a father would.

The Church, too, has given me a structure to love and be loved. I always had, and continue to have, the unconditional love of God. He pulled me through some very dark times.

I was on a yo-yo with Betty. We had been seeing each other for over a year, though perhaps "seeing" is too strong a word. She was dating other men, and from time to time suggested I date others also. But I wasn't tanned and good-looking with a personality that easily endeared me to others. Betty was very popular, and I was only one of many admirers.

However, I believed we had a good and meaningful relationship. We took walks together and went to lunch frequently. We occasionally went to shows and plays and talked on the phone frequently. In mid-January, I had taken her to the American Football Conference Championship between the Cincinnati Bengals and the Buffalo Bills. The temperature was 20° F below zero with a windchill of 60° F below zero. There was nothing romantic about it. I was just glad my car started.

A couple of weeks later I took Betty and two of her children to the Superbowl in Michigan. Cincinnati lost, and I got pick-pocketed. So much for our football dates!

All in all, we had a good time together. The shock of her husband's death was still with her, and she had children to raise. She also had a full-time job. We held hands and kissed, but we were not an official couple.

I prayed about our relationship. I tried my best to be patient and to let things proceed at her pace. It was hard! One moment she would tell me she missed me and wanted to be with me always. Then a few days later, she was dating other men. Perhaps some would have said, "Forget her!"

But Betty meant a lot to me. I had gone out with a few other women after Peggy, but it was Betty who occupied my heart and my thoughts.

Once I asked her if she would like to go to a play with me. She said, "Yes," and I bought the tickets. Then at the last minute she said she was unable to go. I hung up the phone, suppressed my anger, and took my mom. The next day I had to be taken to the hospital with chest pains.

The doctor diagnosed a prolapsed mitral valve, but I knew Betty was also in the equation.

If one would surmise that my romantic life was erratic, at least I could reply that it was solaced by my spiritual life. The doctor said I should avoid stress. Prayer always helped.

I attended my retreats that year with a very special blessing in the form of a dream. I was sitting on the front porch of my house, and as I looked at the sun, it began to come closer to me. I knew somehow that the sun was God, and that I wanted to be with Him. I began to rise until the yellow ball was within arms' length. And then we came together and I felt a joy so intense, so overpowering that in an instant I was awake and jumping out of my bed as if from an electric jolt. I walked about the house in the middle of the night. I felt I had, for a brief second, experienced Heaven.

This was the most powerful and realistic dream I had ever experienced. Its intensity was such that I had no doubts about my faith. I knew Heaven; I had felt it. Now, when I think of my loved ones who have passed away, I am filled with peace and happiness. I know they are with God and feeling the indescribable joy I was allowed to feel for an instant. What a gift God gave to me!

With this experience in my heart, like a treasure, I again offered to serve as a team member for the June singles' weekend. My talk was on vocations: religious, married, and single.

Taking religious vows was a choice. Taking married vows was a choice. Being single was often an unwanted predicament.

In October 1983, I attended a four-day Cursillo retreat and a one-day seminar on "listening." I was trying to discern if I had used the power of choices wisely. In my life, I had tried hard not to lose anything. I wanted to do it all, to get it all --- quickly and successfully. I certainly never had any problem with going the extra mile to achieve these goals.

Then came my experience in Peru.

Betty's deceased husband had a sister living in Peru. Her name was Jean, and she was a Sister of Charity. In 1982, Sister Jean returned to the U.S. for a few weeks, during which time Betty introduced us.

Sister Jean told me of her work among the poor in a shantytown outside of Lima. I shared with her my experiences with the orphans in Oaxaca. I could see in her a total willingness to release herself to God's will. Immediately we were friends. She invited me to visit her in Peru. I told her I would have to think about it.

My last trip to Mexico had not gone well. Just the memory of my illness (we suspected food poisoning) knotted my stomach. And to make it even more of a concern, I would be traveling to Peru alone. I would not be able to speak the language and would be unsure of my accommodations. I wanted to go, but was afraid. I took it to my spiritual advisor. He helped me understand that to know God better, we often have to walk straight into our fears, trusting in God, not ourselves.

I left for Lima, Peru on November 26, 1983 for a nine-day adventure. One of my biggest anxieties had been focused on the arrival at the airport. I worried that Sister Jean may not be there waiting for me. It must have been a premonition, because she was nowhere to be found when I landed. However, I felt a certain sense of peace, and told myself, "Just go with it. Just trust God."

A short time later, Sister Jean appeared, and I was on my way to a slum near Lima called Villa El Salvador. We traveled through the well-lit streets of the big city, and then into the darkness of the shantytown. I stayed awake until 2:00 a.m. talking to Sister Jean and two other women in their convent.

The next morning, the first thing I noticed was the stench outside. The air smelled like the middle of a dump being baked by the sun. I wasn't prepared for the sight, either.

For a man such as myself, having been raised in a small town in middle America, the view was bizarre. There were a few wires looped from pole to pole, to carry electricity to a few of the residents. However, there were no plumbing, sewers, telephones, and garbage collection in sight. There was no pavement and not a blade of grass. There was nothing but dirt. In this dismal one square mile lived 50,000 people!

There were no trees, stores, or restaurants. People squatted in the dust selling a few rank vegetables while sewage trickled just a few feet away. Starved dogs rambled around. Taxis would not venture here.

Sister Jean had one of the few cars in the slum area, and she suffered a flat once a week from the unstable "roads."

When I recall that first morning, I remember filth, and then, oddly, music. I heard the unaccompanied voices of women at Mass. That night the Sisters took me to dinner at the Jesuit retreat house in Lima, beyond the slums. The contrast was striking. Mansions were surrounded by manicured lawns, and luxury cars sat in driveways. Yet we were just a few miles from where I had slept the night before.

The next day the Sisters introduced me to Father Joe. He had lived in the Villa El Salvador for twelve years, and had recruited twenty-six Sisters from all over the world to work with him. Each day, 10,000 people arrived at his church needing food, and, miraculously, he managed to feed them. He was in the process of establishing an orphanage for the many homeless children roaming the streets. When Pope St. John Paul II later visited Peru, Father Joe was one of the people he wanted to meet.

In the United States, we have poverty, but nothing like I witnessed. Most of the people were unemployed, and those who worked made $2.00 per day. On school days, children roamed the streets, barely clothed, begging for a scrap of food.

Yet, in all this apparent misery, despair was not something I sensed. I felt that people in the shantytown took stock of their blessings each day. There was no planning for the future. They let life unfold with each sunrise, wondering what little joys the day would bring. I hoped I could adopt this complacence into my own life. I also learned that faith is our most precious gift. In Villa El Salvador, the people's faith stood out like a shining beacon. It was the only thing these people had, and they treasured it. The excesses of the modern world were absent, and what remained was just God.

Father Joe had said to me, "We'll all be judged not by what we have accomplished, but by what we have given away."

On the first day, all I had seen was the filth of the place. When I said my goodbyes, I felt I was leaving a land of ready-made saints.

Betty and I continued to see one another off and on for a few years. When I began to think of asking her to marry me, I took her to Disney

World, where I had planned to "pop the question." Before I could ask her, I think she sensed what was coming, and she told me that she cared for me, but marriage was not something she wanted with me. She saved me from suffering another heartbreak, by not allowing our relationship to develop into a romance. We continue to be friends even to this day.

CHAPTER 17
SAYING "GOODBYE" TO DAD

It began with a chest of drawers on a cold February morning in 1990. Mom was replacing furniture in my room, and to make space for the new set, she offered my old chest of drawers to the neighbor across the street. The neighbor gladly accepted. Dad first took the drawers out and carried them across the street. Then he hoisted the chest, lumbered awkwardly down the cement steps, and over to our neighbor. It took all of ten minutes.

Over the next couple of days, Dad wondered if he had pulled a muscle during the move. Across his ribs and into the small of his back, he felt a certain tightness. He just mentioned it in passing with a shrug. In his earlier years, lifting rolls of roofing and stacks of tiles over the eves of houses, he had experienced many aches and strains. They had all gone away with time.

But a month later, the discomfort was still with him. Before long, Dad was complaining of not feeling well. My father was a very quiet man and it was unusual for him to ever call attention to himself. For him to complain was something I had seldom seen.

Over the next several weeks Dad just sat around and watched TV instead of partaking in his usual activities. His face was paler and his step more unsteady. He cut back on his forays to Gardner Field and the softball games. He was seventy-eight by then, and over the years his slowdown had been gradual; but now, each day brought an increased level of decline.

I was in the middle of tax season and beginning tryouts for the softball team. Mom and I were both aware of Dad's discomfort, but we didn't dwell on it. Dad was examined by his regular doctor and received a clean bill of health. I just figured my father was getting old.

Our friend, Dianne, suspected something else was happening. The suddenness of the condition, the chronic discomfort, and the fact that Dad would complain; these all suggested to Dianne that it was more than just aging. As only a good friend can do, she pestered us to get a second medical opinion. I relented, and so did Dad. That told me something.

In the spring, I took Dad to a specialist. We spent the better part of a day in waiting areas and examining rooms. Dad reluctantly talked about himself and the pain he had been experiencing. A battery of tests was performed but nothing was found. We were relieved, but to a small degree disappointed. We all knew he was not well, and not finding the cause was disturbing.

Over the past forty-seven years, Mom, Dad and I had developed a pattern of living and loving. We were all essential to one another. We were bound to the many traditions and rituals we had created within our small family. Of course, this was never meant to last. For us, the bell tolled in June, when Dad went to our family doctor again. He mentioned the pain was still there. The doctor ordered a simple chest x-ray, and there it was. Clearly seen, on the sheet of film, were the white ugly splotches of cancer. Further tests confirmed its presence. A month later, Dad was officially told he had terminal lymphoma in the lung and rib area. They told him he had six months to live.

There weren't words to express our emotions. We got through the next few days in a haze. With my grief, I felt a silent, but raging anger with the "experts" who had not detected the cancer earlier. By the time they were discovered, the masses were inoperable. Would the same have been true in April? I tried not to think about it.

In July, 1990, Mom and I took Dad to see an oncologist who concurred that the cancer was terminal, but she said she would do her best to keep it at bay for as long as possible. She ordered chemotherapy treatments immediately. On the way home, Dad said simply, "I'm going to die." Mom and I could say nothing.

Dad continued with the chemotherapy through the rest of the summer and into the fall, going to the hospital twice a week. A lot of his hair fell out, he suffered from chills and often vomited. Just when he had recovered from one treatment, it was time for the next. All through these months, Dad did his best to keep to his routine. Every morning he read the sports page and watched games on TV. With his little radio, he sat on the front porch and watched the activity on our street. He took short walks in the evening and continued to go to Mass each Sunday. At mealtime, regardless of his appetite, he joined Mom and me at the kitchen table.

At Dianne's suggestion, I began attending a cancer support group at the hospital. Most of the people present were family members of those stricken, though some patients would attend the meetings. Dianne and Mom attended with me sometimes, but Dad would have nothing to do with them. I made every meeting. They became a lifeline for me. I realized I wasn't in this alone.

As Dad continued to die a little each day, I think all of us shared a certain heart-felt insight that only a catastrophic event like this can bring to the fore. It's just this: life goes on. Our little world was upside down, but the traffic on the highway just kept moving forward. The world around us was not showing the slightest acknowledgement of the impending loss of one of our most important family members.

Dad was taking one day at a time. As holidays and other mileposts of the year came and went, my emotions were in a balancing act. I was trying to appreciate the moment, with the realization this might be our last Christmas together, the last birthday, the last ball game.

I had tickets to Riverfront stadium for the World Series between the Reds and Oakland A's, but the game wasn't the same for me without Dad. We watched the rest of the World Series together from home.

In December 1990, a tumor was discovered near Dad's colon. In addition to chemotherapy, radiation was now part of our routine. In February, chemotherapy was stopped. Dad had endured as much as his body could stand. Radiation was also stopped a short time later. Dad

Roger F. Grein

felt immensely better, as the effects of treatment had been harder on him than the cancer itself. He knew he wasn't cured, but he appreciated every day.

For his eightieth birthday in March, we decided to have a surprise party for him at the Lockland Fire Hall. Once inside, Dad worked the crowd as I had seldom seen him do. His sisters were there, and all of their children. Dad's buddies were there, as were many of the Sweeney Girls he had befriended over the years. Dad was smiling and clowning for the camera. He opened presents, drank a few beers, and thoroughly enjoyed himself.

It was at this time, too, that Dad began to open up a bit. In the years before his illness, Dad would often opt out of the conversation when friends stopped by. He would sit in his chair in the living room and watch TV. The rest of us would gather around the kitchen table or on the porch. As his sickness progressed, however, he began to join the conversations and really open up.

One incident, in particular, astounds me to this day. Dad had never talked about his Army Infantry days during WWII. I knew he had been stationed in the U.S. for some time and that he had gone overseas in the latter years of the war. That's all I knew, but there was much more to his story. Out of the blue, Dad shared with his friend, Tom, how he had fought in the Battle of the Bulge. He had been pinned down for thirty-one days in a fox hole with two other men. They took turns sleeping, fifteen minutes at a time. All around them were dead bodies. Sniper, machine gun and tank fire constantly raked the area. They were all very afraid. They didn't want to kill anybody or be heroes; they just wanted to get out of there alive. When the tide of the battle at last turned and the Germans were pushed back, Dad and the other men were taken to what passed for a hospital. Their clothes had been on so long, and under such conditions, that they were impossible to remove by hand. Attendants had to use shears to cut them free.

I felt cheated, in a way, because Dad had not shared such experiences with me, his son. But then I reasoned, he had wanted to spare me the terrible thoughts and images of war. It was too painful; too full of evil.

104

He loved me and wanted to protect me and Mom. Through Tom, at last, he had a chance to reveal the horrors he had experienced.

Dad's reprieve began in January and continued for many months. It was during January that my business schedule became hectic, and I knew it would not let up until the end of April. Had Dad continued to decline, I don't know how I could have handled it at all. God had a plan that was best for all of us. I needed to trust in that.

It was during this time, also, that I made the final decision to take the Sweeney Team to the Soviet Union. It was a trip I had dreamed of making for many years; one I had looked into sporadically, but wistfully. Now I had a chance to go.

It was a hard call to make. Dad was well enough in January, but how would he be in July when the trip was to take place? I talked to his doctors and prayed during a retreat to come to the right decision. I knew Mom would think I was nuts, but I was used to that. What I wasn't prepared for was Dad's reaction. He was vociferously opposed. It wasn't my absence during his illness that bothered him. It was the idea of me traveling "behind the lines" into enemy territory. He said, "Anything can happen!" This was 1991 and the Soviet Union was under Gorbachev. Dad believed that anything connected to Russia was treachery. He said that visiting Communist countries was for spies and turncoats; certainly not for his son and young girls.

I moved forward with plans. I understood Dad's point of view, but I saw it as part of the generation gap. There was only one thing that would keep me from going, and that was, of course, the deterioration of Dad's health.

The first week in May, Dad felt pain in his abdomen and lower back. We took him to the hospital. It looked as if Dad's cancer had spread to his prostate and also moved into his hip area. They began radiation again. He was discharged three days later and was happy to be home.

At the end of May, Dad was doing badly and was taken in an ambulance to the emergency room. At that time, I was in Columbus with the team. I talked to the doctors by phone and gave them permission to start intravenous fluids and to take other prudent actions, but not to resuscitate Dad if he began to fail further. I also asked that they not use life support. I packed my bags and left the team with my assistant coaches. Dad's condition had improved by the time I reached the hospital. A week later he had his gallbladder removed.

The hospital wanted to check Dad out before he was well enough to go home, so I had him moved to a retirement center. It was close by and fortunately had an opening. Mom knew some of the staff there and believed it would be a good place for Dad, who surprisingly, accepted the move. He really wanted to die at home, but he also wanted what was best for Mom and me.

A week later, Dad was well enough to berate me again about the trip to Russia. He said he had made a pact with God. He was going to die soon, and knew I wouldn't leave Mom and miss his funeral! It was his way of keeping me home, and, in his view, safe.

The doctors told me Dad's death was not imminent and to make the trip. At that time, I was holding $60,000 in plane tickets and other pre-paid reservations. The girls and I were looking forward to the adventure, so it was still on.

Our softball team competing in Moscow, Soviet Union, August 1991

Of course, Dad was on my mind for much of our time in the Soviet Union. There was no regular overseas phone service, so I wasn't able to check in as often as I wanted. Had there been an emergency, our friend, Dianne, knew how to reach me. I returned to find Dad as well as when I had left him, despite any "pact" he might have made with God.

A few days after my return, Dad was on the phone asking if he could come home from the retirement center. Within an hour, I brought Dad back to our house on Moock Avenue. He joined us for supper at the kitchen table and we were together again.

Over the next several weeks, Dad grew weaker. I took him to a Sweeney game just down the road from our house. I parked by the fence so he could see the game without getting out of the car. The older players that knew him from healthier, happier days stopped by the car window to talk with him.

In September, Dad received additional radiation treatments to ease his pain. On my birthday, September 20, he was able to go out and eat with us, but he couldn't really enjoy himself.

On September 25, Mom fell and broke her wrist. Five days later, Dianne fell and dislocated her shoulder. It seemed my world was falling apart.

At night I would hear Dad moaning in pain. I thought of Job in the Old Testament. I thought of Jesus on the Cross. Both were sinless men, suffering. I wondered, "Why is this happening to my dad? He is a good man who worked hard for so many years, so that Mom and I could have a nice home, and I could receive a good education. Was this his payback?" My faith had never been so tested. I just had to trust in God, but it was a challenge.

I thought of the dream I had had many years before. I still remembered the feeling of the ecstasy of heaven. That would be Dad's reward shortly. I hung on to that thought, and it calmed me.

Mom was tough; much stronger than I. Once, struggling in vain with my awkward hands to open a bottle of Dad's medicine, the frustration cascaded down upon me. I sat at the kitchen table sobbing, still tearing at the bottle cap. Mom snatched the bottle and said, "What's the matter with you?" She had no patience for weakness. She believed becoming emotional was a disservice to Dad and there was no time for it.

In October Dad signed Hospice papers. We had a hospital bed

moved into our living room where Dad could still watch baseball games. Even with medication and the utmost gentleness from his caregivers, the pain had become unbearable. Hospice continued to come every day to bathe Dad and to watch over him while Mom went out for a while. Other guardian angels from the Lockland Life Squad came every four hours to lift and turn Dad. In the spaces of time when nothing needed to be done, Mom sat by his side. Father Carl, from our church, came over and gave Dad Holy Eucharist, heard his last confession, and anointed him with the Sacrament of the Sick. Afterward, Dad beckoned to us. He told Mom he loved her and then he looked at me and said the same to me. It was the first time he had ever verbalized his love to me. Then he added, "Take care of Mom."

On October 29, I decided to take a bike ride. Mom was in the yard raking leaves as best she could wth her broken wrist. I got back a half-hour later. Mom met me at the door and stoically told me, "Father is dead."

Mom had been in the yard when Dad died. He died alone, at home; it had been his wish. Perhaps by being out of the house, we had given him permission to start on his next journey.

Three days earlier Dad had spoken his last word to me. I was on my way to autumn try-outs for the Sweeney Girls' ball team. Dad looked up at me in my uniform and could only manage one word, "Win!"

After they took Dad's body away, Mom finally allowed herself to cry. They had been married fifty-seven years, and her life as a wife had come to an end. I sat with her for a while and then began calling family and friends. Neighbors came over to offer condolences and help. I went down to the hamburger stand close by to get us something to eat and then I picked up our mower from the repair shop. Life went on.

CHAPTER 18
REVELATION PART II

On October 29, 1999, I discovered so much more about my birth circumstances than I could ever have guessed, and I wanted to know more. That rainy morning, when I walked out of the 100 East Eighth office, I was full of excitement. I had learned so much so quickly. I hadn't even had time to process the facts, let alone the implications. It would take weeks, and perhaps the rest of my life, to adequately reflect upon the events surrounding what had happened in 1942. The facts had been obscured by time, and now that they were out in the open again, I wasn't sure what do to with them.

Should I try to find my birth mother, Dorothy? Should I try to find any half-siblings who might still be living? If I did search for them, would I betray an unspoken pact of secrecy? Would I make life difficult for members of my birth family who didn't even know I existed?

On the other hand, didn't I have a right to know my personal history? Was I from German, Irish or Chinese stock? Didn't I have a right to know of any family medical histories that might affect my health? There were no easy answers to these questions. Instead, everything just spun around in my mind. Perhaps it was providential I had lost my voice as a result of my constant cough. I could barely manage a whisper. In the time leading up to the meeting at the Social Services Office, I had been disappointed that I would be limited in my ability to ask questions. As it turned out all I needed to do was listen. If I had found my voice, I would have been too emotionally unsteady to use it.

Now, as we exited the building, Joyce and Dianne couldn't stop talking. Their excitement was as great as mine. Like me, they simply couldn't believe what had transpired. All the facts had been laid out so plainly. My birth parents had lived only a few miles from where I had grown up!

In one respect, I wanted to talk about it, but I was too tired. I needed quiet time to grapple with the facts and see how they fit together, and to plot the next path to learn more about my family.

Joyce and Dianne wanted to keep moving. They wanted to see where the facts might take us, and they wanted to do it that very afternoon. They wanted to go to the addresses listed in the record. Perhaps family members still lived there.

They looked for and found "Robert Wang" listed in the phone book. Was this Dorothy's younger brother and my uncle? Would he remember his sister's pregnancy? What could he tell us?

I kept my mouth shut. I was torn about what to do; whether to go home and reflect and pray, or go on trying to unravel more of the mystery. I decided to follow their lead. I count Joyce and Dianne among my closest friends. The opportunity to be together again at such a momentous time might not be easily arranged, if we were to postpone driving to the addresses we had. I appreciated their presence, and perhaps, I needed their encouragement.

We took my car over to the West Side of Cincinnati. I really did not expect anything much to transpire. It would take more investigation, I was sure. We took the road where Dorothy had lived, but instead of turning left, as the instructions on the record indicated, we had to turn right. Perhaps it was just an error in the notes. The house was supposed to be down the road a mile. About a quarter of a mile, I saw an older couple raking leaves. I pulled into the driveway and asked, "Do you know the Wang family?"

The lady said, "Do you mean Dorothy Wang? I went to school with Dorothy Wang." I was speechless. For the first time in my life, I was in the presence of someone who had looked upon my mother's face.

The woman talked easily, without prompting. She said she didn't know if Dorothy had ever married. She thought her father had a lot of money but never spent much of it. She told me Dorothy's father had died a few years ago, and the farm had been broken up and sold in parcels. She said Dorothy's brother had lived across the street from the old homestead at one time. Then the lady concluded, "I think Dorothy died."

When new facts come at you so quickly, the mundane with the momentous, it's hard to be emotional. Besides, I was still operating under the pact of secrecy I had construed. Unwittingly, a confidence had been placed with me. If my mother had not sought me out, then perhaps she did not want to be sought. I had to respect that. If no one but close family had known about her child born out of wedlock, then what right did I have to reveal a secret she had kept these many years? And even if she had died, that did not give me the right to expose the old secret. I didn't want to tarnish her memory among friends and family. She had refused an abortion and given me life. I owed her.

The lady also told us that Dorothy had no children. I had always imagined my mother had delivered me when she was still a young girl, and that she had probably gone on to marry and have a family. Part of that scenario had been dispelled when I learned that Dorothy was twenty-four years old at my birth. But I still expected to hear she had married and raised children. That was one reason I had not searched for her earlier, and why I was even now anxious not to reveal my identity as her son.

The kind lady directed us back down Thompson and on to Springdale again. The notes had not been wrong. We should have turned left earlier. But now, with the lady's, and God's help, we were on the right track. I could not believe that just a few hours earlier I had not even known my birth mother's name.

The lady raking leaves had told us, "The house is white and has a white shed close to the road. The shed had been turned into a garage for busses."

As we approached the property, we saw a woman in her yard by a white house, so we stopped and asked if her property was the Wang farm. "No," she said, "It's about a half-mile down the road. The Wangs all died and the house has been sold."

Again, my heart sank. Dorothy was definitely dead.

We went to the next white house with a shed out front. It had been remodeled and a pool was in the back. I took a deep breath. This could be the house where my mother grew up. If things had gone differently, I might have lived in this house.

We knocked on the door and a nice woman answered. She said they had bought the house in 1991. She had not known Dorothy, but she knew about her and knew that her brother had lived across the street, but had moved away a few years before. The current home owner invited us in to look around. She said she didn't think Dorothy ever married. She believed that she had died suddenly on a spring day in 1991 on the steps leading to the basement. Dorothy had been cooking bean soup and needed an onion from the basement. On the way down, she fell, perhaps in the midst of a heart attack.

I couldn't cry. There was still the confidence to keep. But I thought to myself, what a terrible way to die.

Not knowing the full impact of what she was doing, this nice lady invited us down into the basement. I began down the rickety, narrow and dark steps. They were difficult to negotiate, especially for me. This was where my mother had died. It was just too much for one day. I mis-stepped and began to fall, just as my mother had done. Joyce was behind me and managed to get enough of a grip on my coat to steady me. I looked back at her with sad irony.

The basement had an ancient and cracked concrete floor that the new owners had covered with an old rug. It was much the same as when Dorothy had been alive. Upstairs there had originally been only four rooms: a kitchen, a common room and two bedrooms.

The current owner mentioned that there were records belonging to the Wangs that had been left in the house. She retrieved the court document dated May 15, 1991 regarding the estate of Dorothy Mary Horner, bequeathing everything to Dorothy's sister, Mary.

I wondered, "Where did the name, Horner, come from? Had Dorothy married after all? Was there still a possibility that I might have half-siblings?"

The lady of the house asked if any of us were related to the Wangs.

Our presence and questions must have seemed somewhat odd. We had not volunteered any information about ourselves and yet were asking the most detailed questions about the relatively obscure, and now deceased, former owner of the house. Dianne and Joyce shook their heads, "No." The lady looked at me. I pointed at myself and said quietly, "I am."

The confidence had been broken, but I had no choice. Everything this day, in this search, had seemed as if directed by God. Everyone we had come into contact with, even by accident, had acted in the most honorable and straightforward manner. How could I now be the least bit deceptive?

The lady did not ask me anything further. I had not admitted that I was Dorothy's son, but the pact of secrecy was beginning to crack.

Then the kind women suggested we go next door and talk to the lady who had been Dorothy's friend. She offered to call and let her know we were on our way.

We walked across the lawn and met Maria. She was a slight woman in her eighties. Her original home had been in Romania. She had lived next door to Dorothy for twenty-six years, and they had been good friends.

Maria also told us that Dorothy had been married later in life to a man who died in 1981. Maria said he had been a good man, and that gladdened my heart. I was happy to know she had found some companionship. Maria also remembered Dorothy's father. He was known as "Pops," and had lived in the house with Dorothy and her husband until shortly before he died. Robert, Dorothy's brother, and his family had lived in the house across the street. They relocated after Dorothy died. Bob Wang and his wife, Helen, had three children; all adopted.

Tears came to Maria's eyes when she spoke of Dorothy. She kept saying, "I miss her so much. She went too soon."

Maria told us about the day my mother died.

Dorothy had been suffering from heart disease for some time, and in the weeks prior to her death, she had felt "poorly." Maria said she particularly worried about Dorothy going up and down the basement steps.

Each morning, Dorothy and Maria would wave to one another from their back porches, just to say, "Hi," and signal that all was well.

One morning Maria missed Dorothy on the back porch and made a note to herself to check on her later. Then, Maria noticed smoke coming from Dorothy's kitchen. Her husband called 911 and the two of them went over to see what was wrong. They found a pot of bean soup burning on the stove and found Dorothy at the foot of the basement steps. There was no pulse.

Maria was crying as she told me this. I did my best to console her.

She began to tell me more about Dorothy. She said my mother always enjoyed being outside and had been an avid gardener. In the summer she would sell vegetables by the road. She also took in laundry and ironing. She went to Mass every Sunday.

I thought that Dorothy and Thelma, my adoptive mother, were alike in many ways. They were both good Catholics and worked hard. I wondered if I would have turned out any differently if I had been raised by Dorothy.

Before we left, Maria showed me a photograph of my mother. She could not have known how impactful this was for me. She did not yet know that I was the son of her friend. I stared at the picture. Dorothy was tall and thin with dark hair. The picture was not clear and I could not make out much detail. But it was my mother; the first time I had seen her.

Maria said Dorothy was buried in the St. James Cemetery close by. Once we said our goodbyes, I got in the car and wondered if my mother had ever confided to Maria about the child she gave away so long ago. If she did, I don't think Maria made the connection to me.

Maria said we should stop at the home of Mrs. Smith down the road for more information about Dorothy. This woman was not home, and the blinds were drawn, so we decided to go to the cemetery.

The rain had stopped and the sky was blue. After a little searching, we found the grave. It read, "Dorothy Mary Horner, April 25, 1918 – April 29, 1991." Next to her was her husband, Owen E. Horner, who was eighteen years her senior.

I could not thank Dorothy now, but, perhaps she was looking down on me from Heaven, and perhaps it had been she who had set this entire day in motion. Perhaps Dorothy had been watching out for me, knowing that now was the best time for the truth to be revealed. How could I possibly thank her? Was prayer enough? Was my love for her in equal measure to the love she had held in her heart for me?

I began to cry. Dianne and Joyce stood on either side of me and hugged me. We said a prayer, turned around, and then I noticed the grave of Dorothy's parents; my grandparents.

All of these discoveries had been made in one eight-hour period of time; one day that changed my life. I felt overwhelmed and went home with so many thoughts running through my head that I couldn't sleep at all that night. I kept reviewing what I had learned that day, over and over.

My day had begun attending a 7:00 a.m. Mass with the Sisters of Notre Dame de Namur. They had agreed to pray for me, as I left to discover my roots. I believe God had indeed answered their prayers.

It had been a day of searching and playing detective. The goal had been achieved, but had I thanked God in a manner befitting to this miracle?

I was reminded of the story of the ten lepers who were cured by Jesus. Nine of the ten, in their amazement and joy, had run off shouting with happiness. Only one, a Samaritan, had taken the time to throw himself at Jesus' feet to give praise and thanksgiving. I identified with the nine, but I wanted to be the Samaritan.

With the information we had, I was able to locate a copy of Dorothy's death certificate. I wanted to tell anyone who would listen, about the sacrifice and unconditional love of this simple woman. I wanted to share her heroism in saving my life.

But in fact, I could not. I still had not revealed my identity. No one in Dorothy's family, or her friends, knew that the child who had secretly been given away fifty-seven years earlier was looking for her! The last thing I wanted was for Dorothy's family and friends to think any less of her, just because of my curiosity. It was best to be quiet and guarded for a while. It was better to review, reflect and pray...and be thankful!

I hadn't said "thank you" to anyone that day. It had all happened so fast. Everything had been led by Christ, I was sure. I now knew I had an uncle Bob and an aunt Helen.

Two weeks passed, while I spent the time digesting everything I had learned. I hadn't, to this point, done anything I regretted. I had found out the identity of my parents, walked in the house in which my mother had lived and died, and visited her grave.

I still wanted to learn more about her. I wanted to know if she had ever thought of me after she gave me away. Any further investigation might risk exposing my anonymity, but if I didn't move forward, I would be left only with speculation.

Contacting my Uncle Bob would be out of the question at this point. I decided the best approach would be talking to Dorothy's friend and neighbor, Mrs. Smith. I thought perhaps Maria, who had been so gracious to us, might introduce us to her.

On November 13, Joyce and I contacted Maria. She told us that Mrs. Smith and Dorothy had been friends for over forty years. She was in her eighties, but was still very active. Maria had already spoken to Mrs. Smith about our visit and inquiries.

Her last comment startled me. Up until that point I had been in control of the investigation. I was able to determine who knew what. But now, people were starting to talk.

Maria told us that Mrs. Smith was more than willing to talk to us about Dorothy. The door, it seemed, was already open. I wondered if anyone had guessed my identity yet.

On the following Sunday, Dianne and I visited Dorothy's friend.

Mrs. Smith told us that Dorothy had been about thirty years old when they became friends. She said Dorothy was slow and had a lisp. She dragged her feet when she walked. *(like me!)* She never drove a car, and after her husband died, she relied on others to take her to the store. Sometimes, Bob and Helen Wang (her brother and sister-in-law) would take her to Mass on Sunday. They also handled her check book. Her husband, Owen Horner, was a quiet man. After they married, Owen moved in with Dorothy and her father. Mr. Horner had no children prior to their marriage, nor did he have any with Dorothy.

Dorothy's dad, Matthias, died at the age of ninety-two. Dorothy's other brother, Arthur, died of a heart attack.

Since the death of her father and husband, Dorothy had taken in laundry, which she would hang in the yard to dry. Other than going to the store and church, she seldom left the house.

Mrs. Smith said Dorothy had kept her home in immaculate condition. She had no air-conditioning and did not own a fan. I again began to think of the similarities between my biological mother and my adoptive mother. The parallels were striking.

Mrs. Smith also remembered how she adored her brother's children. I wondered, "Did she think of me when she played with those children?"

Then, as if reading my thoughts, Mrs. Smith dropped a bombshell. She said that Dorothy had delivered a baby boy who would be about fifty-seven years old now. I was stunned. How did she know? Mrs. Smith, by her own account, had not met Dorothy until five years after my birth.

Then Mrs. Smith said that after Maria had phoned her, she in turn had called Bob Wang to inform him that someone was inquiring about Dorothy.

"Well, then," I thought, "The cat's out of the bag." Bob was still in the home when Dorothy was pregnant. Certainly, he had put two and two together and figured out what was going on.

Instead of anxiety or guilt, I felt relief. Now it was incumbent upon me to make contact with my Uncle Bob and to let the whole truth come out. It wasn't a bad truth. I simply wanted to know my mother and the circumstances of my birth. Aware that Bob had adopted children himself, I felt certain he would be open to meeting me.

A side, but important issue, in the pursuit of my family history was the matter of genetic health conditions and how heart disease kept raising its ugly head in their lives. Dorothy had suffered from a bad heart and her brother, Arthur, had died of a heart attack at a relatively young age. Maria told me that Bob had recently recovered from heart surgery.

What did all of this mean for me? I wondered if I had inherited a weak heart also. Dorothy and Arthur had all died when they were about ten years older than I was when I discovered this new family. The thought sobered me. I thought to myself, "Well, if there is something you have always wanted to do, Roger, you'd better get busy."

I also knew that the most important spiritual goal is to have one's soul pure and ready for God. Whenever my time is up, it's up, and a quick heart attack might be a welcome way to die.

Soon after that visit, Joyce and I called Robert Wang's home. This was to be an important call; the first time I would make direct contact with a member of my biological family. I said a prayer before dialing, and was at peace with however things turned out.

Helen Wang, his wife, answered the phone. Her voice made me feel comfortable immediately. She said that Bob did not hear well, and was no longer able to use the phone. She asked if I was a member of the family, so I told her I believed I was. She also told me that Dorothy's sister, Rose, was still living just a few miles away. She said she knew that Dorothy had delivered a baby in September or October of 1942, at which point I said, "I was born September 20, 1942." Helen immediately invited me to come to her house. She said Bob and Rose would both love to meet me. It was a done deal. We scheduled to meet November 19 at 1:30 p.m.

I asked Joyce and Dianne to accompany me, as they had been with me every step of the way throughout this odyssey. I wondered, "Would conversation be easy? Would there be some pain involved? Would the Wangs recognize my disability as a part of their family heritage?" Joyce and Dianne could help me with conversation and be there for me if my composure started to crumble. They agreed to be by my side.

My uncle and aunt lived in a beautiful ranch home. They greeted me with hugs, and without a word, all pretense about my identity melted away. Looking at me, Robert said he never dreamed that this could have happened; that he would meet Dorothy's child. Then Rose and her husband, Earl, arrived; then two of Robert's adopted children came through the door. It was a wonderful family reunion - more than I could ever have imagined!

Robert corrected some facts for me. He said that Dorothy was the oldest child, and that Lillian Wang, my grandmother, had delivered five children, not four. The last baby had lived only one week before dying of "spasms." They all told me that Dorothy had shuffled her feet, and that she had stuttered most of her life.

Robert said that Dorothy was mentally slow and hard-headed. She was a good cook, loved to bake and tend her garden.

The family believed that Dorothy never told her husband, Owen, about her earlier pregnancy. Dorothy had suffered a miscarriage early in their marriage and she never conceived again. Robert Wilde (pronounced Wildee), my biological father, had come from a family involved in the nursery business. They described him as tall and dark-haired. He was known for his beer drinking and was a Jehovah's Witness. They thought he might be deceased.

At one point in our discussion, Bob and Helen brought out some family pictures. They all said Matthias, my grandfather, walked with a limp and I reminded them of him. I agreed. There were also many pictures of Dorothy. These were the first clear images of her that I had seen. Helen Wang kindly offered to have prints made of any of the photos I wanted.

Dorothy Wang Horner, my biological mother

As our family reunion continued, the conversation became comfortable. They said Dorothy never mentioned me to anyone. That was understandable. The pregnancy had been an embarrassment for the family. No one ever discussed the pregnancy before or after I was born. Dorothy had been a heavy woman in her twenties and the pregnancy wasn't apparent, so no one in the community ever found out her secret.

But --- a lady named Emma knew. She was not part of the family. I wanted to know more about her. Helen said that Emma had lived next to the Wangs for many years, and then moved to New Mexico. She had not been back for ten years, but they stayed in touch. Emma usually called Helen and Robert about twice a year just to say, "Hello."

Incredibly, Emma called as I was sitting at the Wang's kitchen table! I nearly jumped out of my seat. What a miracle! Helen handed the phone to me, and I was told the story of my conception.

Emma told me that she was often put in the care of Dorothy's grandparents (my great-grand parents), John and Mary Wang. She attended the wedding of Matthias Wang and Lillian. Emma sometimes babysat Dorothy, who was about ten years her junior.

Eventually, Emma married a man names Jules and they lived with Emma's mother. Emma said, "Dorothy would keep her younger brothers and sisters in line, but she was mentally slow."

When Dorothy had grown to be a young woman, Jules became acquainted with Robert Wilde. They would often ride to work together. Soon, Dorothy and Robert began seeing one another.

Emma told me that two and a half weeks after the Pearl Harbor attack, on Christmas Eve, 1941, I was conceived in a nearby hotel called the Flicker Inn.

Sometime in February 1942, Robert brought Dorothy to Emma's house and asked Jules to drive them to the Doctor's office. Emma came along with them and waited while they went in a back room. She heard Dorothy say, "Oh, it can't be!"

The next day Emma called the Doctor. He told her that Dorothy was pregnant. He also told her that Robert and Dorothy wanted an abortion, but that he would have nothing to do with it. He had recommended putting the baby up for adoption.

Later that day, Dorothy asked Emma for a ride to the drug store. She said she needed some medicine to relieve her stomach cramps. Emma started asking probing questions, and finally, Dorothy admitted she was pregnant. Robert Wilde had told her the "medicine" she was going to buy would cause a miscarriage. Emma told Dorothy, "There is a life there. You can't kill it." Mr. Wilde had told Dorothy that it was not a child, and that she would not be killing a baby. She would only be taking "medicine" to make the pregnancy go away. Emma refused to take Dorothy to the drug store.

When Mr. Wilde came by in his car, Emma told Dorothy to stay in her house. Then she went outside, raised her fist, and told Robert Wilde to get off her property. Robert's face turned purple with rage and left.

Emma was small but fearless. She was a practicing Lutheran, and had a strong faith in God and the value of life. She reminded Dorothy of her Catholic faith. She asked Dorothy if she was really prepared to commit murder. Dorothy said, "There is no life here yet. Robert said so." Emma said, "Dorothy, you have a child inside of you. It's alive and if you do what you are planning to do, you will commit murder."

Dorothy appeared scared and did not know what to say. "It is a sin," Emma continued, "Abortion is a sin." Emma would not let her do it.

Dorothy considered Emma to be her best friend, and she agreed that she would not go through with the abortion.

The next morning Emma walked the half-mile to Dorothy's house and found her in the basement doing laundry with her mother. Emma then told Lillian what had happened the day before, and Lillian nearly fell over the wash basin.

According to Emma, once Lillian learned of the pregnancy, there was never a question that the baby would not be born. And there was never any question who would pay the doctor and hospital bills: Robert Wilde, my biological father! And he did!

Later, Robert Wilde told Jules, "Emma blew the whole thing!" And that was true. Had it not been for Emma, Dorothy would have made it to the drug store, and by that evening, I would have been dead.

As Emma relayed all of this to me over the phone, I cried and then she cried. I thanked her as best I could and hung up. I said my good-byes to my uncle and his wife, and departed for home. The next day I called my travel agent and inquired about flights to New Mexico.

Only two months earlier, I had begun my journey to find my biological parents. Now, I was going to meet the woman who had saved my life. Just a short time ago, I had no idea my life had ever been in jeopardy. Now, I knew an abortion had been planned by my father and my mother. Thanks be to God; Emma had intervened.

Prior to my departure to New Mexico, I had an unexpected call from my cousin; the son of Rose, my mother's sister. He was friendly and told me that as a boy, he had spent his weekends with Dorothy. They played cards together, and she had mentioned to him that she had given birth to a son, and that she always wondered what had happened to him. So, my mother DID think about me! That was very comforting to know.

New Mexico was a different world from my home town of Lockland, Ohio. As we landed, I could see mountain ranges and scrubby pines. On the ground, the brown of the earth, and the dryness of it, was overpowering. It was obvious I was in a desert.

Emma's son and wife met me at the Albuquerque airport. He had a sign that said, "Welcome, Roger." With his infectious smile, the sign was superfluous.

As we drove to Emma's trailer, I marveled at the wilderness passing by. It was so foreign to me. It was a miracle that my life had been saved, and now I was going to meet my savior.

Emma stepped outside of her small trailer as we pulled up. I walked over and up the steps. I am over six feet tall and Emma was less than five feet. I looked down at her and smiled. She had been crying. I was ready for the moment. I had worried that my "thank you" would be terribly shallow considering what this lady had done for me. My first words to her were, "You saved my life." She looked up at me and said, "There's the boy I saved. I never thought I would get to see him."

We sat on her couch and I held her hand. She began to tell me everything that had happened. Most of the information was the same as she had told me over the phone.

I learned a few more things. Emma had been living on the brink of poverty, struggling to raise two children and take care of her mother. Most people thought her meek, yet when the plans of the abortion became apparent, she stood up and stopped everything. She was a 4'9" Goliath! In a way, she gave me the maternal protection that my biological mother, in her panic and misunderstanding, had not.

My heart was filled with gratitude and love for Emma and Dorothy. My impression was that they both had been resolute in their faith. I construed that Dorothy would have raised me herself, had it not been for her impoverishment and the shame of an illegitimate birth. I tried to look at things objectively and without judgment. Emma remembered Dorothy as a simple farm girl, who was naïve enough to be led astray by someone of questionable character.

Emma learned from Lillian that Dorothy was conscious during my birth, and when the doctor took me to her, she covered her head with the sheet. When I started to cry, she covered her ears so as not to hear. Lillian, too, turned her head away and walked from the room. That was my entrance into the world.

I can never be sure, but I believe by hiding her eyes and covering her ears, my mother's actions demonstrated how hard it was for her to give me away. For my grandmother, too, the pain was obvious. She knew the sacrifice would have been harder if she had looked at me. I was able to forgive them both.

Emma had kept these secrets for fifty-seven years. She had just turned ninety when we met. On the day of my departure she said, "God saved you. I didn't. He just used me."

I like to think Dorothy was smiling on me from her place in Heaven, and that she was happy I was discovering more about her life.

I flew back to meet Emma three more times before she died. I called her my "princess," since she had saved my life so many years before. We became good friends.

Regarding my biological father, Robert Wilde, I bear no ill-will. I can't explain why. After all, this is a man who never showed me love, who instead planned for my abortion, and was angry when Emma thwarted his plan. I wonder what qualities I inherited from him. Did he ever think of me?

A few years later, in 2003, I discovered that my birth father *was* still living. I found him residing in Indiana near South Bend, 250 miles from my home. I decided to drive there and visit him, unannounced.

I walked up to his house and rang the bell. When Robert opened the door, I said,

"Hello. I am your son by Dorothy Wang." He was stunned and hesitated. His wife, Cookie, was in the kitchen and heard my voice. She came over and extended a welcome. If she had not opened the door to me, I'm not sure Robert would have let me in.

He had told his wife, years before, that he had fathered a child by Dorothy, but he didn't know if she had given birth to a son or a daughter. He also didn't know if his child was still living.

As we talked, they told me that they had married in 1943, and sadly, were never able to have children. They had recently celebrated their 60th wedding anniversary. Robert had been born in 1917 and was eighty-six years old when we finally met. While we were talking, Cookie's niece, Rae, came by for a visit. She was shocked when they introduced me, as she had never been told I ever existed.

I continued to visit them both until their deaths. I am still in touch with Rae.

Robert Wilde, my biological father, and his wife, Cookie

In February, 2024, I took a DNA test. The results showed my heritage composition to be: 48% from Germany, 23% from England and Northwestern Europe, 22% from Sweden and Denmark, 4% from Scotland and 3% from Wales. There is not a drop of Asian blood in the mix! Perhaps an overworked clerk at Ellis Island changed Wagner, or Wangerin to Wang. Your guess is as good as mine! But it was fun to find out.

CHAPTER 19

SAYING "GOODBYE" TO MOM

Dad had detected it first. Out of love for Mom, however, he said nothing. Like a sailor feeling the slightest waft of trouble in the air, he knew a storm was brewing.

I saw the signs, too, but had failed to read them correctly, or to even see them as contributing to a major medical issue. There were little things: a strange blank stare, an uncharacteristically poor play in a card game, a checkbook error. I excused these lapses as a part of aging. Mom was in her seventies, after all.

While my father was dying, Mother was the strong one, despite these frightening behaviors. But the thief that had been lurking in the shadows had already arrived. From his death bed, Dad saw the signs. Mom had been present for my father, marshalling all of her reserves on his behalf.

"Take care of your mother," was the last complete sentence he spoke to me. Dementia snatched my mother in 1992.

After Dad died, her behavior became even more bizarre. Mom ran the car through the hedges. She bought six boxes of salt in as many weeks. She answered, "Hello," when the phone rang on a television show. The sad part was, she was aware of this decline, so with this clarity came depression.

In September 1992, Mom turned 79. She agreed to a geriatric evaluation. Our friend, Dianne, went with us for moral support. After a three-hour evaluation, the Doctor said that Mom had Alzheimer's disease. He said Mom should give up driving immediately. He told her she should not be left alone, and she would have to give up cooking. He suggested I move her into an assisted living facility as soon as possible.

I had not expected such a drastic diagnosis. Mom glared at the doctor, her lips tight and her expression icy. I knew she expected me to stand by her, the way she had stood by me when I was sixteen and was told not to drive. Mom still had her dignity. She understood what all of this meant; the report was a threat to her world. After all, her home was her kingdom, and she was still the ruler. Mother was determined <u>not</u> to do what the doctor had prescribed. We left the clinic silently.

I look back on that day and thank God for Dianne. She loved my mom, but she was removed enough to know what should be done. As soon as we were alone, she gave me some good advice. She said the car keys had to be taken away and the stove disconnected. "You will never forgive yourself if you don't do these things, and then something terrible happens," she warned.

I didn't question her advice, or the doctors, but I did not have legal power of attorney for Mom. Worse, there was the unspoken, but always present knowledge within me that neither the doctor nor Dianne would understand our history together. This woman had accepted me, defects and all. I was not of her blood, and she could have returned me to the orphanage and in my place have been given a boy who could function normally. But she did not; she never even considered it as an option. She rubbed my feet and legs until her hands ached. She endured the questions regarding what was wrong with me. My mother had been alone through all of this, while my dad was far away fighting a war. She knew there was a good chance he would never return from that war, but she kept me just the same. Now she was counting on to me to help her through this trial. I could not just shut her away in an assisted living facility, no matter how much sense it made to the outside world.

I was scheduled to go on a retreat soon, and I debated whether I should go. When I made the decision to leave, Mom still had the car keys and was still cooking on the stove. I prayed to God for help and intervention. I asked that He give Mom the help she needed because I didn't have the guts to implement the doctor's orders.

I came home from the retreat on Friday. On Saturday morning I was in my office when the police called. My mother had been in a wreck with the car. The policeman said Mom was unhurt, but that I was needed at the scene. She was in the back of the police car when I arrived. Her car was totaled and had to be towed away. The accident had not been Mom's fault, but I could see this incident was an answer to my prayers. Mom was scared. I told her the car could not be repaired, and I knew her mind was clear enough to recognize that she could not learn how to operate a new automobile. Thanks be to God; she was off the road without an argument. Perhaps the rest would fall into place just as easily. I prayed for more help from God.

After the accident, Mom began to talk about living in a retirement home, but only if she could be the one to make the decision. Before agreeing to this, I was determined to learn all there was about Alzheimer's disease. If I knew enough, I thought I might be able manage the situation on my own. I enrolled in a support group for family members living with someone suffering from the disease. One of the things I learned was that the caregiver had to tend to his own needs in order to care for the loved one. In this area, I had been failing. My concentration was pulled in too many directions, and I had two accidents in rapid succession; one with my car, and one on my bike. I hurt my leg in the first accident, and suffered a concussion with the second. I recognized I needed more help.

Time went by. Mom still took care of the house and I cooked. I took care of the shopping and errands and stayed as close to home as possible. Mom would call me six or seven times a day at the office, forgetting that she had called me earlier. The only constants in her life were her home and me, and I was not doing well.

The bad times were increasing and the good times were fewer and fewer. Mom could not keep dates straight, and I would find her on the corner waiting for a bus that would never come. I had to acknowledge that Mom was no longer the person who had raised me. I knew, that for her best interest, I had to either put her in a nursing home, or provide for around-the-clock care in our house.

At the end of 1993 I took Mother over to the St. Clare Retirement Community to look at a two-bedroom independent living apartment.

She was completely opposed to it. I considered home care, but I knew she would not allow a stranger to run her home and cook in her kitchen. So, I put off the decisions once again.

By spring of 1994, I knew something had to change. I considered selling my business and quitting softball to stay full-time with her. But just as God had answered my prayers before, He seemed to be giving us another gift – just in time.

Mother came down with a bad cough. Her doctor saw the cough as a means to initiate some movement out of our house. He told Mom she should check into St. Clare's Retirement Community for a recuperative visit, all-the-while knowing that she may end up being there for the rest of her life. Mom, not seeing his ulterior motive, agreed to go.

The next morning, she awoke coughing, and she reminded me of the appointment at St. Clare's. She packed a bag with her belongings, made my breakfast, gave me the newspaper, made my bed, packed my lunch and off we went. She had been in our home for almost sixty years, and this was the morning of her departure.

Mother, in this new setting, could not fathom where she was and what had happened to her. Nothing was familiar. Her bed was not familiar, there was no kitchen in which to cook, there was no front door to lock, and the faces around her were those of strangers.

When we first arrived, she walked through the front door without trouble. I escorted her to the sixth floor and to her room. I kissed her on the forehead and left. The process had gone smoothly and was, I thought, nothing short of a miracle.

Later in the day I went back to check on her. By that time the miracle had evaporated. Mother sat on the edge of her bed, clutching a packed bag and waiting for me. When she saw me she became hysterical. She grabbed my arm and begged to go home. After a few meaningless assurances, I separated myself and walked quickly to the elevator. As the door was closing I saw nurses and aids restraining her. It was the worst moment of my life, and I think of hers also. She knew she wasn't there for a cough.

In three days, Mother's condition plummeted from a confused, but semi-rational person, to what seemed like a woman with complete dementia. Guilt washed over me anew.

My visits were never easy, and I came to dread them. The staff suggested I not visit each day, but I knew in my heart I had to be present, regardless of the consequences. I often shriveled at her fury, but learned to accept it. At one point she said, "I'm going to come back and haunt you when I'm dead."

One time I came to see her and no one could find her in the building. I finally located her at the edge of the property, walking toward the street. I pulled my car beside her and took her back to our house on Moock Avenue. She walked from room to room and then walked over to visit a neighbor. Then she told me she was ready to go back to St. Clare's. She walked through the entrance as if nothing had happened.

She began helping the staff with small chores, such as folding laundry. She made her bed and kept her room tidy. Each Friday I would take her back to our house so she could touch base with her old life.

In the Fall of 1996, she began to decline even more. At about this time, I found a note she had written in early 1992, when she was becoming aware of her dementia. She had placed the note in the back of one of my drawers. She talked of her belongings, and to whom she wanted them given, and then she tenderly added, "I know it will be a terrible change, but you can work it out. I think Jesus will help you get through the hard times. It won't be easy." I put the letter in my pocket and read it often. It was a great comfort for me.

For years I visited my mother twice each day. I got to know most of the residents and staff through my frequent visits. I became part of their community.

I would start each day at 8:00 a.m. Mass at St. James, then I would head to work for a few hours. Next I would drive to St. Clare's, eat my bagged lunch and use the exercise equipment at the retirement center to work off my tension. After a visit with Mom, I would leave for work again, and then return later in the day to bid her good-night.

After Christmas of 1999, Mother did not recognize anyone except for me. When I came for a visit, she would say, "That's my baby."

One day in June of 2003, I heard the song "Amazing Grace" being played as I approached her room. She passed away right after that song ended.

The following poem, "The Chosen One," was read at her funeral Mass. There wasn't a dry eye in the church.

"The Chosen One – Thelma Grein"
A Poem by: Anne Brennan CSJ & Janice Brewi CSJ

The day she brought her Roger home, Thelma
stayed all night with Frank,
Drinking in, drinking in her blue-eyed baby boy.
Eight years of longing, longing bound her to that crib,
A thread - God spun - a path that shaped her life.
This destiny - this child alone - the One to make
her Mother; for this she came, chosen.
This one of all earth's children, this one boy, her holy call,
This one would call her forth.

"Take him back," they cry, "first steps are not right."
All alone, Frank gone, away at war, she faces them alone.
Love held her ground. Love grounded her.
She rubbed his legs, she urged him on, and up, and over hills of can'ts.
"Heel-toe, heel-toe," she chants. "Heel-toe, heel-toe."
Sunk deep beneath his feet, soul deep, it firms him still.

She pushed and cheered, determined him.
"Just wait, you'll climb the cherry trees of life,
But at your own pace, unhindered, limb by limb."
She sent him higher, day by day, as God knew only Thelma could.
Others might have told him, "You can't."
She freed him with her strength, her grit patient.
Pacing him to run with kids, to school with friends.
To work with drive, to pray with hope, to college too, to love
To love without strings.
"Heel-toe, heel-toe," she knew he could and would.

"A car?," they said. "Drive?," they said, "Never!," they told her.
She handed him the keys.
"You failed," they said. "Don't work at that again."

131

"Nonsense," she said.
She pounded out the numbers. She typed him to the top.

God knew her well; fierce, trusting one.
Patient, supporting in every way.
Patterning the feet, legs and heart of a child
to carry him through life.

Tough tenderness, undaunted, choosing, Chosen one.
Endlessly urging us all, "heel-toe, heel-toe" at our own pace,
At God's pace. One step at a time. Thelma's gift to the world,
A man for others, a people for others, a woman for others.
God calls her once again, one last path.
"Mother, welcome home."

In memoriam: Thelma Grein, June 15, 2003

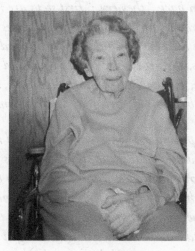

Thelma Grein, shortly before she died

Two weeks after Mom died, I turned on the car radio. The song's lyrics repeated, "I know when you go to heaven, the angels will look after you."

It gave me peace.

CHAPTER 20

THE PUBLIC SPEAKER

Some might say that the start of my public speaking avocation was serendipitous. I think the Holy Spirit led the way. It started with a simple dinner in May 2004.

The Dominican Sisters of St. Gertrude in Cincinnati invited me to dine with them, and as we ate a modest meal, they shared their conversion stories with me. I, in turn, told them stories from my life.

The following September, one of the sisters I had dined with was transferred to Nashville. She lived at the Dominican motherhouse and taught in a high school nearby. She asked me to come to her school and speak to her students.

That made me pause. At times, my cerebral palsy causes my tongue and lips to move in uncontrollable ways, and I have trouble pronouncing certain consonants. Ironically, the word, "philanthropy" is one of the most difficult words for me to say.

So, when asked to talk publicly to classrooms full of teenagers, I wasn't sure I would be able to make myself understood.

I'm not a shy man; quite the opposite. I make friends easily, but speaking to a group, without an interpreter, and without the means of making sure I was communicating clearly, was quite another challenge. It would be like trying to breach an eight-foot wall without a ladder. I said I would have to pray about it. I talked to my spiritual director, and reassured by his guidance, I agreed to give the talk.

I was scheduled to give nine talks, over the course of three days, to

133

the high school students in Nashville. I also spoke before seventy-five novices and postulants while I was in town.

A few days after returning home, I received letters of appreciation from the teenagers. It was very gratifying and also a relief. The children seemed to understand my message and appreciate my visit. I believe God had a lot to do with the success of my talks.

In February of 2005, I was asked to be the keynote speaker for a fund raiser in St. Susanna Parish in Mason, Ohio. That was also received well.

In the Fall of 2005, I was invited to speak to a group at St. Ann's Church in Fairfield, Ohio. Erin Campbell, a local radio personality, was present for this event and approached me after my talk. She asked me to be a guest on her radio program, "Water Through the Word." A CD entitled "The Mower Boy" was developed from that interview; over time I distributed 20,000 copies of that CD.

I have learned that when you say, "Yes" to God, you'd better put on your seat belt!

Some of the talks I gave were unplanned. For example, while I was in Florida staying with a friend, we attended morning Mass. After the service, I met the celebrant, Father Nick, and gave him one of the "The Mower Boy" CDs. The next day, my friend and I we were attending a fund-raising event at that same parish. The scheduled speaker didn't show up, so Father Nick asked me to fill in for the key-note presentation. My talk was off the cuff, but by then, I was getting the hang of speaking to a crowd.

Another incident occurred while I was visiting a friend in Illinois. I stopped for Mass before heading home. It happened to be the first day back to work for teachers of the parish school. They were attending the same Mass as my friend and I. Before leaving, I introduced myself to the principal and handed her my CD. During the course of that conversation, she asked me to be the keynote speaker for their staff that day.

St. Mother Teresa's order, the Missionaries of Charity, invited me to Washington D.C. to share my story with fifty of their sisters. While in that city, I also talked with AIDS patients in one of their facilities. After that talk, the Mother Superior requested that I travel to New York City to address their sisters of the same order. In New York, the Sisters suspended all of their activities on the day of my talk so that 150 members could attend.

Once "Magnified Giving" was organized, I addressed several groups of students each month to promote our program.

In total, I have made presentations to various groups over 1,000 times in eighteen states in the U.S.

Things slowed down during COVID, but invitations to speak picked up again after our schools returned to normal activities.

In 2024 I visited St. Henry's Catholic School in Northern Kentucky, where 440 children were assembled. During our question-and-answer session at the end, one of the youngsters asked me, "Did you ever receive a trophy for your philanthropic work? If not, Jesus should give you one."

My answer was from the heart. "I have received more gifts from God than I ever deserved or could have imagined."

Please link to the documentary below to learn more about my life's journey.

<u>www.rogergrein.live</u>

CHAPTER 21
ALMOST IN THE MOVIES

After the documentary about Pete Rose, "4192: The Crowning of the Hit King," was completed, I attended a special premiere for it at the Esquire Theater. The year was 2010.

The producer and director of that documentary were both in attendance. I talked to the producer, and asked if he would be interested in making a movie of my life. I gave him a copy of "The Mower Boy" CD and my business card.

He eventually commissioned a movie script to be written based on my life. I was invited to the Phoenix Event Center in Cincinnati for a "table read," with actors playing the parts of me and others in my life. My friends, Tom and Dianne, shared this incredible experience with me. I was overwhelmed. My life unfolded before me. The producer then gave me a copy of the script to take home. I read it that night.

I thought how blessed I was to have such an experience.

The script was taken to Hollywood soon after that, and was pitched to a major movie company. They were interested, as long as I would sign over my total rights to them, to do as they pleased with the script. My attorney looked over the agreement and told me that if I signed the document, I would be giving the movie company permission to change the script in any way they wished. They could warp my life to make a sensational movie, and I would not have any recourse.

I did not sign the contract.
So much for my Hollywood experience!

Maybe someday, another studio will be interested. One never knows what wonderful things God has planned!

CHAPTER 22

PHILANTHROPY AND MAGNIFIED GIVING

I learned the value of giving very early in life. After I had saved enough money from my pop bottle returns and newspaper recycling, I would buy gifts for my mom and dad. It gave me great satisfaction to see them open their small presents, purchased with much thought, and great love.

A movie about the life of St. Francis of Assisi also inspired me. St. Francis taught me that living a simple life and helping others provides a satisfying sense of fulfillment to the giver, and it is pleasing to God.

An example of how I carried out the mission of giving occurred early in my career. I had just started my tax business and had $1,500 in my checking account. At that time, a representative from a local charity, stopped by my office and asked for a donation. I gave him a check for $1,000 to support the non-profit organization. Many people would think that I was being foolish, but I trusted in God. I knew if I would do His will, and say "Yes" to his promptings, everything would work out.

Later in life, after getting my first glimpse of true poverty in Mexico, I began donating money to the orphans in the City of Little Children in Oaxaca. I also helped our softball team raise money to buy gifts for the little boys living there. It was a good life lesson in philanthropy for those high school girls. We traveled to the orphanage and gave them love and hugs, as well as toys, clothing and food. I continued to return to their city over the years, bringing them both necessities for their survival and hope for a better future. As time went on, little girls were welcomed to the City of the Little Children.

In considering my softball girls' futures, I donated money to Northern Kentucky University to support their collegiate softball program. This provided scholarships for my high school girls, and for many others, preparing for their careers. In honor of these scholarships, the softball field at NKU is named after my father, Frank Ignatius Grein. I also provided scholarships in my mother's name, Thelma Louise Grein, for physically and mentally challenged students attending NKU. Over the years, I probably donated close to a million dollars to NKU.

Furthermore, in honor of my birth parents, I sponsored one house for "Habitat for Humanity" in Dorothy Wang's name, and another house in Robert Wilde's name. Altogether, I donated three houses to that charity, as I also contributed our family home on Moock Avenue, when I moved out in 2018.

I was always looking for ways to help the needy folks in my local communities as well. When I would see a notice in the newspaper about a shoe store or toy store going out of business, I would buy the last of their remaining inventory and give the shoes and toys to local charities. When I read in the newspaper about a house that had burned down, and the family had no money or insurance to rebuild it, I went to the bank and withdrew money from my account in the form of a certified check payable to the family to use for rebuilding their home. The family never knew where the money had come from. This style of giving was repeated many times.

Over a period of many years, I donated in excess of $12,000,000 to my local church, through a Donor-Advised Fund, which in turn, wrote checks to local charities. Those local charities never knew the money came from me, as the checks were written from the church's account. I always wished to make anonymous donations. After all, the thanks should go to God, not to me.

In August 2001, I learned about a new method of philanthropy. During a luncheon meeting with the president of Northern Kentucky University, I learned that the Mayerson Foundation targeted money for student programs to award grants to charities. Through this program, the college undergraduates were challenged to make tough decisions regarding which group or charity would be awarded the funding. The concept of the students making the decisions and conducting the research excited me. It was the power of multiplication! It got me thinking.

Soon after that lunch, I attended a retreat in Milford. During that retreat, I met the retired president of Xavier University. After I shared with him the conversation I had had with the NKU president, he arranged an appointment for me to meet with the acting president of Xavier.

At that meeting, I agreed to donate $4,000 for a class to award grants to specific charities, and $1,000 to compensate the instructor for the extra work required. The students could distribute the money as they chose: one charity could get the entire $4,000, or they could split it up among other non-profit organizations.

This idea was implemented at Xavier in 2002. At the end of the term an award ceremony was held to announce the grant recipients.

While I listened to the students' reports of their research and decision-making process, everything came alive for me! At the conclusion of the program, I was honored to present the checks to the charities. One student remarked to me afterwards, "This was the best thing I've done in four years!"

At that time, there existed an organization called a "Campus Compact." This was a national coalition of colleges and universities, that incorporated service-learning into their curriculums. Their programs were similar, but students provided service rather than money to the non-profits they had studied. I met the President of the Ohio Campus Compact at that time. Through him, I met many other college presidents in Ohio and Kentucky. In 2003, the program that was piloted at Xavier University expanded to Wright State, Mt. St. Joseph, and Thomas More Universities.

As more schools came on board each year, I would travel to tell my story, and pledge money to support the program. The formula stayed the same: I donated $5,000 per college per year.

By 2008, seventeen colleges and universities were involved in the philanthropy program.

Before the financial crash of 2008, I had seven million dollars invested in bank stocks. I thought banks were safe. In July, a financial tsunami hit! I lost all of my investments except for $65,000. I hadn't been diversified. I was left with nothing with which to grow my portfolio back; nothing to recover my losses.

Not only had I been pledging money to the colleges, but I was also donating a lot of money to other charities. I gave money to my church each year, and they were counting on those contributions. I was giving away about $700,000 each year, which included my mission work and trips to Mexico. All of this went rushing through my mind. What was I going to tell all of those people who were counting on me?

I cried like a baby. I was sixty-six years old!

I took stock of what I had left: my small two-bedroom house in Lockland (which I had inherited from my parents), an IRA, and a business that I had been planning to liquidate. After all, it was time to relax and enjoy life, right? But I still had many friends, my health, and most importantly, I had my faith in the Lord. God had always loved me and cared for me. I believed that was never going to change, and that He would help me through this crisis.

The first thing I did was visit many college presidents of the schools to which I had pledged money. I apologized because I could not continue to donate to their programs. I didn't want to just send them a "Dear, John" letter. Some of the presidents told me, "We will continue this program, even without your donations, because this learning experience is too important to our students."

Encouraged by the success of the past programs, a federal grant was requested and awarded to the universities in the amount of $2.97 million dollars! This allowed the universities and colleges to carry on the experience for the students. They became self-sufficient. This was gift from God!

That Christmas of 2008, I sent out 3,000 cards with my holiday greetings. I asked for donations to expand the philanthropy program, which I had christened "Magnified Giving." The first year we accepted $13,000 in donations. The second year we raised $22,000. That base continues to grow with contributions from our community businesses and individuals. This has been another gift from God.

In 2010, an eight-person board was formed to oversee the Magnified Giving program and we became a 501(c)(3) non-profit organization. We were operating from my tax office at that time, and growing quickly. In the Fall of 2015, the board decided we needed more room.

We found a deserted building on Reading Road. It was a mess, but I was told it was good structurally and could be salvaged. One of the board members said, "You will need a million dollars to buy and renovate the building." I said, "We better start praying."

Again, God answered our prayers. Joyce Kupfer-Mulderig made a pledge of $100,000 per year for ten years, for a total of one-million-dollars. This was donated in honor of her parents, John and Jean Kupfer. The donation was earmarked for the purchase and maintenance of the building to house the Magnified Giving offices. Because of this generous gift, donors' contributions will not be used to cover building maintenance, but can go directly to the program grants nominated by the students. The building is also made available, without charge, for the use of non-profit organizations within our local communities.

By 2016, thirty-five high school and middle schools were involved. Magnified Giving had an executive director, an office manager, and twenty people serving on the board.

The board developed this Mission Statement:

"To educate, inspire, and engage youth in philanthropy, and to touch the hearts and minds of teens, lighten the concerns of others, and magnify the impact of philanthropy."

As of 2024, we are operating Magnified Giving programs in approximately 136 sites such as high schools, middle schools, the Girl Scouts, Juvenile Detention centers, and youth groups. We also offer a summer camp, "Camp Give," that teaches students in grades 5-9 about philanthropy. Between 2008 and mid-2024, we have granted $1,780,426 to 640 nonprofits through the hands of youth. These numbers continue to grow.

We are collaboratively merging businesses, private donors, and schools, while the needy in our communities are benefitting. When we work together, following God's Holy Will, we all thrive.

Two testimonials:

My name is Julie Ciocci, and I'm a manager at Ernst & Young. I have known Roger for ten years; from the time I was a student participating in Magnified Giving's programming, to now sitting on the Board of Directors for Magnified Giving.

Roger has made a significant impact on youth through the development and growth of Magnified Giving's Youth Philanthropy Program. Launched by Roger in 2008, the Youth Philanthropy Program enables students from grades 6-12 to learn about philanthropy and explore what it means to be a philanthropist. At the end of their program cycle, the students select a nonprofit to which a donation is awarded. It is significantly important to highlight that it is **the students who are the decision makers.**

We often think about philanthropy as how adults choose to donate their money. However, we cannot forget the fact that we have the responsibility to guide future generations on how to give back to their communities. By providing our youth with philanthropy education and empowering them with strategic decision making, we are empowering them to be more insightful and thoughtful servant leaders as adults. Roger's work with the Youth Philanthropy Program has so far empowered over 45,000 students over the course of sixteen years.

I am one of those 45,000. In 2015, I participated in my high school's youth philanthropy program as our Student Program Director. This opportunity provided me the ability to engage professionally with nonprofits in my area and gain a strong understanding of my community's needs. I also began building a close relationship with Roger and the Magnified Giving team. This ultimately led me to study Organizational Leadership at the University of Cincinnati, with the end goal of wanting to make a difference in the business world.

Since then, I have volunteered at Magnified Giving regularly, served as an intern helping to develop our summer "Camp Give" program, and now I sit on the Board of Directors. Professionally, I voluntarily serve on our corporate social responsibility team at Ernst & Young in Chicago, driving relationships and volunteer efforts with our nonprofit partners who specialize in sustainability efforts. It is unlikely I would have traveled down this path if it were not for the commitment and efforts of Roger Grein and Magnified Giving.

Roger Grein's dedication to the youth has not wavered, as he continues to share his story and passion with students, ensuring they are provided the education and opportunities they deserve. He is a remarkable individual who inspires me every day to be a better version of myself and to leave the world a little bit better than I found it.

Sincerely,
Julie Ciocci

As a teacher at Perry High School, I have had the privilege of working closely with Roger through his Magnified Giving program, witnessing the profound impact he has had on my students and our community.

In 2008, Roger started the Magnified Giving program to teach high school students the art of philanthropy. What began as a small nonprofit that supported philanthropy education at eight schools in the Cincinnati area, has grown to include over 136 schools and youth programs throughout Ohio and Northern Kentucky. My association with Roger Grein dates back to 2013 when my Perry Service-Learning students joined the Magnified Giving Program.

Admittedly, I was skeptical when Magnified Giving's director approached me at a high school service-learning conference and asked, "How'd you like it if I gave your students $1,000 to grant to deserving nonprofits in your community?" It sounded too good to be true. Typically, if I want to raise money to support educational initiatives for my classroom, it requires my students to turn into salespeople hawking candy bars, magazines, or raffle tickets. But Magnified Giving is anything but typical.

The success of Roger's program stems from its simplicity. Magnified Giving provides schools and youth organizations with $1,000 and empowers students to nominate and award grants to nonprofits. In addition to providing partners with an engaging curriculum that guides students through every step of the philanthropic process, Magnified Giving also introduces students to Roger. For many years, he made the journey from Cincinnati to Cleveland, sharing his inspiring story of philanthropy with my students. Post-pandemic, we have continued to be inspired by the documentary found at the website: www.rogergrein. live. This has become a powerful substitute for his in-person visits. Through his interactions and the documentary, Roger instills in my students the invaluable lesson that the secret to living is giving.

The hands-on experiences that my students have had as a result of Roger's vision have been nothing short of transformative and have created a ripple effect of positive change. Since 2013, my students have awarded over $22,000 to local nonprofits through the Magnified Giving program. The impact on my students' lives is immeasurable. Each year, I witness them using this program as a platform to recognize and support nonprofits that have made a profound difference in their lives or the lives of their family members. Students facing personal challenges, such as loss, mental health struggles, poverty, or family members battling illnesses, find a voice and a means of support through Magnified Giving. Regardless of which organization ultimately receives the grant, every student emerges as a winner.

Sincerely,
Mark Soeder
Director, Perry Service-Learning Program

For more information about our 501(c)(3) non-profit charity:
www.magnifiedgiving.org

FINAL THOUGHTS

Q&A from various interviews:

Q - If you could go back and change anything in your life, what would you change?
A. - Nothing. The setbacks I experienced made me who I am today. I learned a lesson from each challenge.

Q - What social causes are the closest to your heart?
A - I feel called to support education to the uneducated, and provide food to the hungry.

Q - What is your life's purpose?
A - To love and to be loved. And to gain everlasting life in Heaven someday.

Q -What are you most proud of in your life?
A - I'm most proud of working with youth. First as a coach of high school girls' softball for almost 40 years, and later establishing <u>Magnified Giving</u>, which teaches youth how to give their time, talent, and treasure back to their community. In both roles, as a coach and as the founder of a high-impact, mission-driven nonprofit organization, I have exposed youth to the world around them, and helped them to be aware of people and issues, that they may never have known before.

Q - From your experience, what is most important in life?
A – Faith, family, and friends. Contentment, health and protection.

Q - What do you believe in?
A - God and the goodness of other people.

Q - What is the one thing you need to do every day to get ready to take on the day?
A - Pray. Get in touch with God. Pray for others and their needs. Have a PMA: Positive Mental Attitude.

Q - What is one defining moment that changed the course of your life?
A - Getting fired from my job at a bank. It was my first job out of college. I worked in the trust department doing taxes. They said my writing wasn't clear and that I wouldn't progress in the organization. But that was a blessing, because it led me to start my own business as a tax accountant. It changed the course of my career and my life. If you're passionate about what you do, you'll never work a day in your life.

Q - What difficult situation happened to you that, in hindsight, turned out to be a blessing in disguise?
A - In 2008 I was substantially invested in the stock market, but I had not diversified my investments. I lost over $7 million when the market crashed. I also lost my ability to be a quiet angel who funded dozens of educational programs that I had committed to help support. I went through the five stages of death. It caused me to reflect on what was really important in life. Faith. Family. Friends. But, because of the loss I suffered financially, I was motivated to reach out to others to join me in supporting the many charitable causes I cared about. It humbled me to ask others to join me to continue work that I had started. I wrote over 3,000 letters and sent them to every person I had ever met. To my total delight, they joined me to turn my dream into a reality. I didn't know it at the time, but the darkest time of my life actually led to my greatest joy - *Magnified Giving.*

Q - When was a time your beliefs were challenged?
A - My beliefs were challenged when my father was suffering from cancer and my mother had Alzheimer's. I had to let go and trust in God, even though I could not understand why good people have to suffer.

Q - How do you find fulfillment and balance in your life?
A - Through prayer and caring for others, through family and friends, and I balance that with self-care and exercise.

Q What do you want your legacy to be?
A - I want people to remember me as a good person. Kind, gentle, and generous. Hopefully that is transferred through *Magnified Giving* and through many thousands of students who will be touched by the spirit of philanthropy for generations to come.

We are all called to pass on love. Many people have loved me throughout my life. Some loved me enough to give me life; some loved me enough to give me a *good* life. God gave me His love and the grace of perseverance to help me handle rejection and overcome obstacles.

My advice to you, the reader, is to turn to God when you are despondent. Know there is a time for everything. God's timing is perfect; trust in that. You are significant and valuable; never forget that. Bloom where you are planted.

Do Small Things With Great Love.
- Mother Teresa

Magnified Giving is institutionalized now and it will carry on without me. Perhaps, some of the budding entrepreneurs involved in this program will take my place, and continue the pattern of social concern they have learned as I did so long ago.

I hope and pray that this program will educate, inspire and engage students in patterns of generosity. I want it to touch the hearts and minds of students, lighten the concern of others, and magnify the impact of philanthropy. That is my goal. That is my legacy.

For more information and photos of my life, watch a 39-minute documentary posted at the following web site: www.rogergrein.live

Proceeds from this book will be used to support the Magnified Giving 501(c)(3) non-profit charity.

POSTSCRIPT

Awards and Recognitions

(Note: Roger was reluctant to include this section in the book. His humility was bothered by the immensity of it. Each time we worked through a draft, he would direct me to "delete these." Those with whom I shared drafts agreed with me that it is important for the reader to be cognizant of many of the accolades Roger's local communities awarded to him over a life of giving. Claire Patterson)

The father of one of my softball players bounded into my tax office. He smiled and said, "Roger, congratulations. You are going to be the 1988 recipient of the Hutch Award!" I just had to look at him. Was this a joke? The Hutch Award was for the likes of Paul Brown, Joe Nuxhall, Waite Hoyt and Sparky Anderson. It was for people at the professional sports level. I was certainly aware of what had been accomplished by the Sweeney Girls, but I had never dreamed my work would catch and hold the attention of a nominating committee who, as far as I knew, recognized only professional sports figures.

The Hutch Award was named for Fred Hutchinson, a Cincinnati Reds manager who, in the midst of his career, was struck down with cancer. The award is dedicated to sporting figures who hold the values of Fred Hutchinson and who are involved with youth. The award was coming to me! It was hard to believe.

The ceremony for the presentation was scheduled for Memorial Day at Riverfront Stadium, just prior to the Reds-Pirates game. It was only three weeks away. I looked at my calendar. There was a conflict. I had planned to be in Columbus with the Sweeney Team for a set of important games. I called the tourney organizers and they told me there was no question about it; I had to be at Riverfront. They rearranged the schedule, and my girls played eight games in one day! The following day, most of my team was in attendance for the award presentation, although we were all exhausted, and many had sustained injuries during the very long day of play. We wore our green and white Sweeney uniforms and we stood in a semi-circle near the pitcher's mound. Tens of thousands of people were in the stands.

When the award was presented, I walked to the microphone, wondering if my voice would hold or if I would succumb to tears. I winged a short speech and looked at my team. In the stands were my parents and my friend, Betty. The girls stood around me as they presented the award, and we all cried. They knew how much I loved them.

A summary of some of my awards and achievements are listed below:

6/19/1964	Bachelor of Business Administration - the University of Cincinnati
6/19/1966	Master's Degree in Business Administration - the University of Cincinnati
11/13/1969	Registered as Public Accountant - Accountancy Board of Ohio
1978	World Championship Tournament Win – Sweeney Girls' Softball Team

Our World Championship Team! I'm standing on the far right.

1982	Outstanding Youth Softball Manager - Sweeney Chevrolet and Buddy LaRosa
1985	Service to Mankind Award - Tri-County Sertoma
10/1986	"To Roger Grein, in Honor of Your Generosity and Companionship" – Catholics United for the Poor
1986	Community Service Award – Catholic Big Brothers and Sisters
5/29/1988	Fred Hutchinson Award for Outstanding Contributions on Behalf of the Youth of Greater Cincinnati - Savings and Loan Association of Southwest Ohio
5/29/1988	Proclamation by Mayor – "Roger Grein Day" in The City of Reading for His Work With Youth, His Respected Tax Business, "He has come to be an individual whom everyone in the community loves and respects."
1990	World Champions Salute to Roger Grein - Red's Riverfront Stadium
1993	Hudepohl Softball Hall of Fame: Manager Category
	Overall record: 2,100 wins and 500 losses
	33 National and World Tournaments,
	21 Top Ten Finishes, 1 win

1995	Human and Spiritual Values Award – Reading Kiwanis Club
1995	Services to Mankind Award – St. Rita School for the Deaf
1997	Special Award for Coaching Girls Softball since 1964 - Hamilton County Sports Hall of Fame
1997	Community Service Award – Catholic Big Brothers and Sisters of Cincinnati
1997	Entrepreneur of the Year Award – Reading Chamber of Commerce
11/18/1999	Identified as "The Quiet Angel," after donating $387,000 to Northern Kentucky University
1999	Entrepreneur of the Year - Reading Chamber of Commerce
4/6/2000	Dedication of Frank Ignatius Grein Softball Field - Northern Kentucky University.
4/30/2000	In Recognition of and Appreciation for Outstanding and Long-Term Service, Commitment and Contribution - Women's Sports Foundation. (Note: over 36 years, Roger coached and/or managed an excess of 3,000 games.)
8/6/2000	Anchor of Hope Award - Hope Lutheran Church
11/18/2000	Distinguished Alumnus Award - Lockland High School
2000	Long Term Service and Appreciation Award – Greater Cincinnati-Northern Kentucky Women's Sports' Association
2001	Certificate of Appreciation for Continuing Support of Inner-City Students – Archdiocese of Cincinnati
2001	Charter Member, Santa Maria Circle of Friends
2002	Founder of "Student Philanthropy Project" (changed to "Magnified Giving" in 2008)
8/7/2006	Certificate of Appreciation from The Health Care Connection - Lincoln Heights Health Care Center

2006	CISE Campaign for Students – Appreciation Poster from Eight Community Schools
5/12/2007	Doctor of Public Service, Honoris Causa - Chatfield College
12/2/2007	Santa Maria Community Service Award
9/12/2008	Dedication of Grein Field – Lockland High School
2010	Longevity Award - Reading Chamber of Commerce
11/15/2012	The Father George Mader Award - Catholic Volunteer Network
2012	Ohio American Justice "Cheerful Giver Award" – University of Cincinnati
2012	"Philanthropist of the Year" – Association of Fundraising Professionals
2014	"Voices of Giving" Award
7/7/2016	Commissioned as Notary Public by Governor John Kasich of Ohio
2017	Inducted into the Hamilton County Sports Hall of Fame
2017	Youth Philanthropy Service Endowed Scholarship in honor of Roger Grein – Mount Notre Dame High School
2018	Southwest Region Friends of Education Award – Small Business Administration
2019	Transformation Award – Center for Respite Care
2019	Nelson Schwab, Jr. – Distinguished Alumnus
2019	Participant in 100th Reds Opening Day Parade – Roger attended his 64th consecutive opening day activities
10/18/19	Award in Recognition for Building Community Partnerships to Advance the Education, Health and Well-Being of Others – Guiding Light
2020	MUSE Creative Award and Gold Winner
2021	"Best Inspirational Film" - Top Shorts Award

2021	"An Empowering Philanthropist" by Bob Kelly - The Telly Awards
2021	Plaque in Honor of Five Years of Service to DePaul Cristo Rey High School
2021	Non-Profit of the Year Award – VonLehman Firm
2022	Jefferson Award for Outstanding Public Service – Rotary Club of Cincinnati
1971-2007	Countless trophies for the softball teams. "I don't think any youth team ever accomplished what we did. We played in 33 National Tournaments and finished in the top ten of 21 of those. We won one final World Championship in 1978."
4/24/2024	Making an historic trip down the Grand Canyon

I'm in front of the sign getting ready for our descent.

I'm in a special chair, enjoying every minute!

9/2024   The University of Cincinnati honored Roger by naming a new service-learning award presented to nonprofits who work with UC students as they serve as co-op interns while in school. It is called *The Roger Grein Award for Community Impact.*

10/3/2024   YMCA Keystone Award in the category of Relationships for 2024: "Your dedication and contributions to our community have not gone unnoticed, and this award is a testament to your outstanding efforts."

OTHER BOOKS BY
CLAIRE ANN PATTERSON, M.ED.

<u>Through Mary's Eyes</u>: This is an engaging story about the final days of the Blessed Virgin's life on earth. During those days, she tells others about her son, Jesus. She answers questions such as: How did John the Baptist survive the slaughter of the innocent babes? Why did an obedient twelve-year-old son leave his parents for three days? How did Luke, who was not a Jew or an apostle, know so much about Jesus? Why was Jesus reluctant to perform the first miracle at the wedding feast of Cana? What did Mary experience while Jesus was being scourged? What did Mary do after Jesus ascended into heaven?

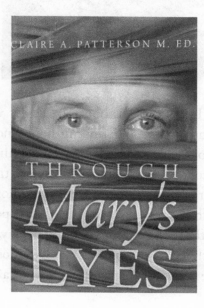

<u>Finding Grace Through Mary's Eyes:</u> This memoir chronicles the story about how Duke and Claire Patterson's lives were changed as a result of heavenly intervention. It relates the events of their lives before, during, and after their first pilgrimage to Medjugorje. Duke experienced inner locutions and apparitions from Mary, the Mother of Jesus, and from other heavenly visitors. These messages brought them both blessings and challenges.

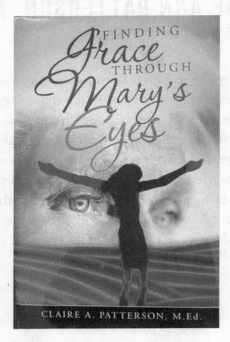

<u>All Who Will Listen:</u> In this book the reader will find stories of overcoming loss and doubt, and finding hope and faith. There are stories about occasions when God, His angels and saints, have interacted directly with the contributing authors in critical times of need. The reader will find stories from more than thirty authors of various faiths and ages, but all with the same goal; to share their experiences of struggle and triumph with those who need to find hope, joy, and direction for their lives. The authors are normal people; like those you meet at the grocery store, those who cut your hair, repair your air conditioner, and

teach your children. These are people who sometimes struggle to pay their bills, deal with family difficulties, and love to sleep in. They are regular people who, through God's grace, have received guidance, cures, and answered prayers.

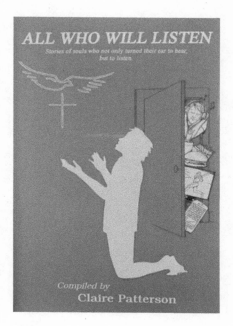